THE STORY OF GOD AND HIS PEOPLE

TEACHER'S GUIDE

Deanne Vollendorf

AUGSBURG PUBLISHING HOUSE
Minneapolis

Contents

Introduction 3

The Old Testament

1. The Story of God's Love, Part 1 6
2. Promises, Promises 9
3. In the Beginning 12
4. Trouble in the Garden 15
5. Tracing the Promise 24
6. The Great Escape 28
7. You Shall Not 31
8. The Conquest of Canaan 34
9. Three Kings and Two Prophets ... 37
10. The Big Split 40
11. Gloomy Prophets 44
12. Hope in the Midst of Disaster .. 47
13. Living in Hope 50
14. The Survivors Return 53
15. Stories, Songs, and Wisdom 56
16. The Time Between 59

The New Testament

17. The Story of God's Love, Part 2 65
18. Death to King Jesus! 68
19. Long Live King Jesus! 71
20. Get Ready for the Kingdom 74
21. Follow Me 77
22. Now Hear This! 80
23. Who Do You Say that I Am? 83
24. Chosen to Serve 87
25. Hail to the Chief 91
26. It's a New Day 94
27. Dangerous Business 98
28. Friend or Foe? 101
29. Hang On to the Gospel 104
30. Who Can You Trust? 107
31. Free! Free! Free! 110
32. The End? 114

Individualized Instruction 117

Retreats 122

CHOSEN

The Story of God and His People

Prepared under the auspices of the Division for Life and Mission in the Congregation and the Board of Publication of the American Lutheran Church.

This Teacher's Guide is accompanied by a Student Book, *Chosen*, by Daniel J. Simundson and David L. Tiede.

Design by Koechel Design.

Photos: Ewing Galloway, page 49. Almasy of Three Lions, 92.

Copyright © 1976 Augsburg Publishing House   All rights reserved

Manufactured in U.S.A.   2 3 4 5 6 7 8 9

Introduction

What we are about

This course is written to provide an interpretative survey of the Old and New Testaments. The student's book can be a textbook for congregations in their confirmation ministry and it can also be a resource for use in the home. The teacher's guide is written to provide background information and teaching suggestions for the classroom, along with individualized instruction and retreat helps.

What we aim to do

It is important to keep in mind specific objectives or goals for the course. This study can be an exciting adventure. There isn't a more powerful story anywhere than this one about God and his chosen people. And just as any great adventure has many interesting details, ours does too. That is why we must be careful to keep the central objectives in mind, so that they remain foremost in our planning and teaching.

The central objectives of the course are to help the students:

- get an overview of Scripture, both Old and New Testaments.
- see the Bible as the story of God and his love for his people.
- see themselves as God's people, chosen and loved by him.
- come to know the people in the Bible as real flesh-and-blood people like themselves.
- sense the centrality of Christ throughout the Bible's story.

These are the things we want to keep in mind as we plan week by week. Each lesson will have many interesting points to discuss, but you should keep one main objective as the heart of each lesson. This concentration on the central objective will be helpful to you as you choose from the several options found in each lesson.

Course overview

The emphasis in this interpretative survey is on following the exciting story of God and his chosen people. The Old Testament lessons trace the covenant history of the people of Israel, beginning with Abraham and moving through the key events of the exodus, the kingdom, the exile, and the return. The key word is covenant or promise. The New Testament lessons follow the main events in the life, death, and resurrection of Jesus, followed by the story of the early church in the lives of Peter and Paul. The key words here are the cross and the resurrection.

How we plan to do it

1. **Materials.** Your students will need a copy of the reading book, an RSV Bible, and a notebook. You may want them to choose a looseleaf type like your teacher's guide so that things can be added or taken out. It would be helpful if it had a pocket for keeping projects and quizzes.

We suggest that the basic reading in the Bible for this course be done in the Revised Standard Version. This is an accurate translation which gives the foundation necessary for understanding the survey of the Old and New Testaments. Paraphrases are not recommended for direct study; if you wish to use them as supplements, use the RSV first to establish the meaning of the text. For a simpler translation we suggest Today's English Version.

As the teacher, you will want to have a copy of the student book along with this guide. Since the guide is looseleaf, you will be able to make it your notebook as well. Just add pages of new ideas and projects wherever you like. And remember to make use of the wide margins for notes.

2. **Background information.** This will come to you in several ways. This teacher's guide will provide the basic information you need in planning your lessons. There will be times when you may need to use outside resources such as Bible dictionaries and commentaries. Don't forget to make use of resource people like your pastor and other teachers and acquaintances. Plan to dig in whenever you need additional help. Make use of your church library, the public library, or some other helpful resource.

3. **Supplements and aids.** Check into the availability of filmstrips, maps, and other helps that your church may have. Make use of as many things as you can which appeal to the senses. Sometimes a picture, a recording, or an art object can vividly illustrate the main objective of a lesson.

4. **Methods and activities.** This guide suggests many things you can do in your class to appeal to some of the varied interests of junior high people. With careful planning and choosing, you can make these lessons come alive.

There are many more activities than you will have time for in any one class period. Read through the entire chapter before planning your session; then choose the activities that fit your situation and the amount of time you have. Keep in mind that you can include more activities if you divide your class into small groups and let various groups work on different activities.

Choose activities you feel comfortable with, but don't be afraid to try something new. Be yourself. Allow yourself to think in terms of what the lesson goals are, where your students are, how they respond to certain things, and especially what you as a group do best. The students will catch your spirit of enthusiasm. Of course there are times when things appear to go badly in the classroom. Remember that such experiences are normal for every teacher.

5. **The Bible.** Our purpose is not to substitute the student book for the Bible, but rather to let it lead us into the Bible. You will find that each lesson takes you directly into the Bible. The aim is not to simplify the story but to put it in the context of the story of God's chosen people. Use the Bible every week. You can give Bible reading assignments for home or use them as part of the lesson in class, but emphasize that the Bible is the heart of our study. In it we find the message of God's love.

6. **Personalize.** In order to communicate with these young people, they must know that you care about them. Throughout the course, demonstrate God's love for people by the love you show these young people. The story of God and his people in the Bible is the story of God and his people in your class. Get to know each one. Much of what you communicate will be "caught and not taught." Your life will probably be the best object lesson they have.

It should be emphasized that although this guide offers a step-by-step teaching procedure, it will be necessary for the teacher to choose from the many activities suggested in each lesson. Do not attempt to do everything! The activities are different ways of achieving the same objectives—pick those that will work best for you.

A word about eighth graders

Chosen has been written with eighth graders in mind. It can, however, be used equally well with seventh or ninth graders, because each age level includes individuals with greatly varying characteristics.

The junior high years are a time of great growth and change in a person's life. Because the student enters junior high as a child and emerges as a young adult, these years are both challenging and frustrating to students and teachers.

The students you are about to teach will in many ways reflect behavior at both ends of the junior high scale. They will at times be surprisingly mature in outlook and attitude; at other times they will react childishly to themselves and the world around them.

Because of the wide differences in physical and emotional development, this age presents unique opportunities for both teaching and learning. The teacher who can approach the eighth grade class with a spirit of adventure and openness will do much to help the experience be a successful one for all concerned.

Physical development. For most students, the eighth grade falls at age 13 or 14. Boys at this age are generally experiencing spurts of growth; they look and feel ungainly in many respects. Changes in body, complexion, and voice add to their discomfort with themselves. By this age most girls have reached complete physical maturity; they are often preoccupied with their outward appearance and with the appearance of others. Teachers can help students most at this age by understanding and accepting both appearance and the behavior it may lead to with humor and love.

Behavior. Eighth graders in general have a poor self image due to physical and emotional changes. In many ways this is an age of self-consciousness, moodiness, and self-concern. There is great need for privacy and time alone. At the same time, however, a person of this age is cautiously open to new experiences and relationships. There is also a tendency toward greater independence, something which parents and teachers often see as rejection and therefore view with great alarm. Yet such independence is in many ways a healthy sign, for it indicates that the young person is reassessing his or her role in relation to peers, adults, and self.

The teacher who can provide opportunities for testing and experimenting within a structured, secure framework will in general find the eighth grade class an exciting and satisfying group. The most successful teacher will be the one who can help students to accept themselves as having value within the community and can lead them to accept others in the same way.

Learning needs. While younger persons are content to gather information about a subject, or about the world, eighth graders are actively seeking opportunities to put what they have learned into practice. They are concerned more about their relationship to God than they are with facts about him. They need to see a clear purpose in all that they do, especially within the classroom, and must feel that their activities and efforts are appreciated and worthwhile. They are capable of carrying much responsibility, yet need help in setting goals and determining plans for reaching them. All students at this age, however, react positively to being treated in a more adult manner within established limits, for they are beginning to think about themselves and the future in a more mature way.

Within the classroom, the most successful discussion questions will be those that give the students a variety of clearly defined choices instead of asking for open-ended responses. Abstract concepts need to be discussed in specific, personal ways. Discussion and activity should be blended in order to appeal in some way to every class member.

Perhaps the best way to deal with the eighth grade student is for you to stop, look, and listen. Each individual is developing at a different rate and each class will seem to have its own style and character. Your ability to relate to your students is enhanced by the time you can spend listening to what they are saying, showing interest in them as persons, and accepting them as valuable members of God's family. If you can watch them as they get involved with each other, listen to their questions and problems, and let them know you care for them, you will come to understand eighth graders and love them as individuals. In return they will come to trust you, return your interest and learn to care about you and what you are trying to say.

Abraham's World

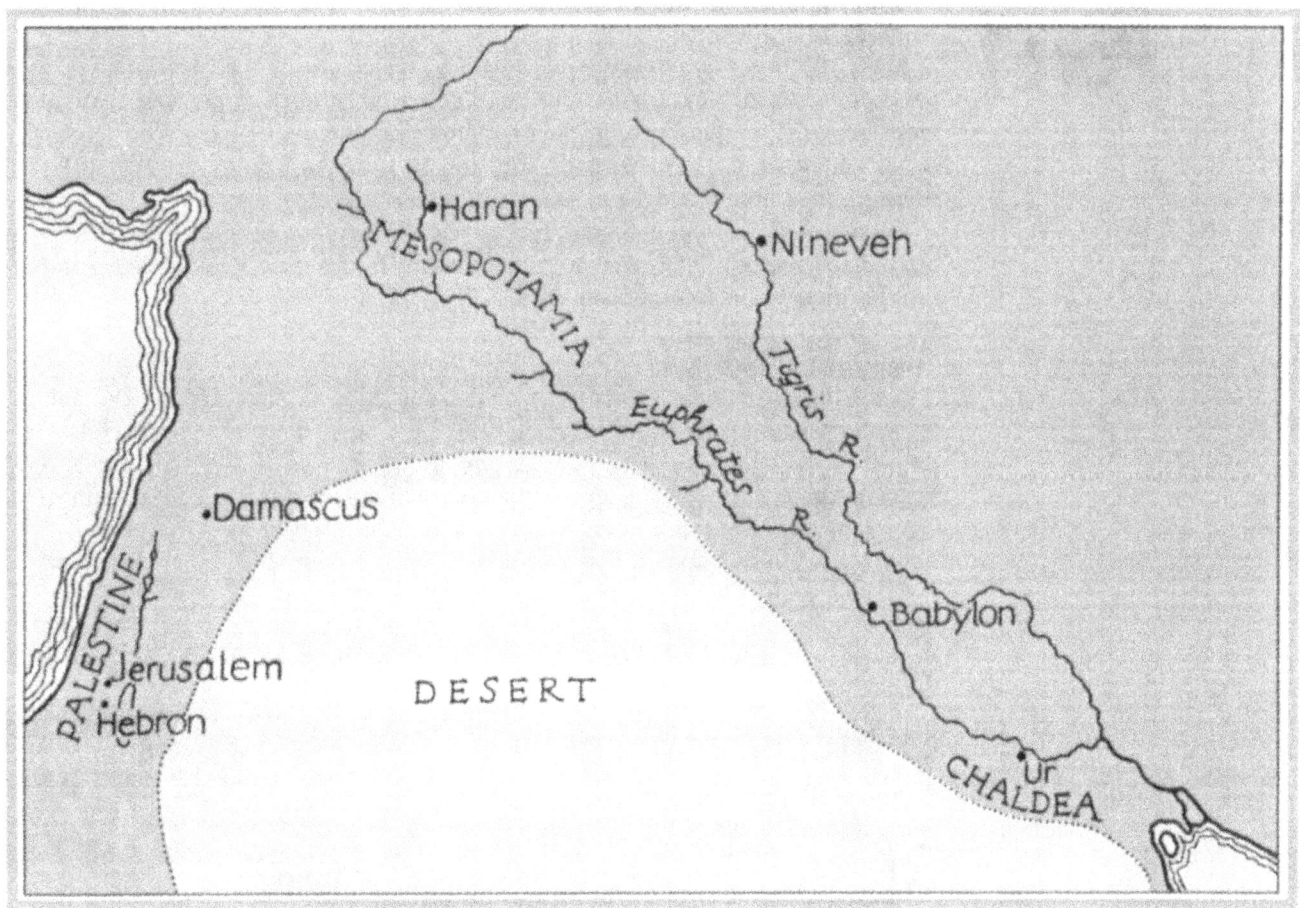

The Story of God's Love

Part 1

Objective
The objective of this lesson is to get acquainted with your students and to introduce them to the theme that the Bible is the story of God's love.

Background Information
This will be the first meeting with your new class. Make it count. Reread the course objectives and the age group characteristics for your class. You need to do two things in this first meeting:
1. Begin to get to know each other.
2. Present the course theme—God in his love has chosen a people (Israel) and a person (me).

Set the stage for a good class by first making sure that all have copies of the student book and an RSV Bible. Then study the first chapter of the student book, keeping in mind that the Bible is the story of a particular people and their understanding of God. It conveys a divine word in a human setting.

Preparation for class
Everything should indicate to the students that you are excited about what is going to happen.

Make the room as attractive as possible. Select one thing they will see as a focal point when they arrive. This could be a large map of the Old Testament world or a list of questions on the chalkboard about the course (*Who wrote the Bible? What is its main theme?*) Use this as a starting point to talk with students as they come, and as a way to introduce the first lesson.

Have a page in your notebook for names of class members and use it to keep attendance records. This will help make them aware that you think it's important for them to be present each time.

The lesson experience
Allow time for your students to chat informally as they arrive. Do not assume they know each other, even if they have been in confirmation classes together in the previous year. Unless the group has been together for several years, prepare some kind of get-acquainted activity. It need not be complicated. You could start by introducing yourself and telling where you live, and a little about your family, hobbies, and interests. Then ask your students to do the same.

Or you could divide the class into groups of two and ask them to interview each other with the idea of introducing their partners to the class. The emphasis is not on how well one does but on establishing basic relationships with each other.

You might want to make up some starter questions like "The funniest thing that happened to me this week was . . ." or "My favorite dessert is. . . ." This would help put the students at ease and get them ready for more serious work. And you might want to consider using name tags for at least one week. They can be helpful for everyone in the class. Have them make a name tag with a simple symbol telling something about themselves.

Remember that they are probably wondering what you are like, just as you have your own concerns about them and how they will like you. Try to set an atmosphere of openness, excitement about being together, and mutual sharing. Sharing feelings about what we expect from each other can be a good beginning for a class. So let them know what you are like, what you expect from the class, and what they can expect from you.

Use the Bible. After this get-acquainted time, turn to the Bible, pointing out that our purpose is to study it to discover what it has meant to other Christians, and what it means for our lives. You might begin with a short devotion from

Psalm 121. After reading the psalm, offer a prayer for your work together as a class. Soon you will want to assign class members to lead in devotions at some point in each class, using Scripture passages from the lesson being studied.

Introduce the student book. Encourage your students to page through the student book, noting chapter titles, pictures, and maps. If they have previously received their books, perhaps they will already have read the introductory chapter. But don't assume they have!

Allow time for silent reading, or ask for volunteers to read aloud for the class. This is not a good time to request each student to take a turn—poor readers are placed in a difficult position because they are not yet comfortable with the class.

This is the time to establish whether you intend them to read the chapters as a home assignment each week or if this will be done in class. A short explanation of what you expect in the way of class preparation will let them know the pattern they will be following from week to week.

Have them keep their books open so you can refer to certain paragraphs during the class discussion.

Discuss what the Bible is. Ask what comes to mind when they think of the Bible. Is it the family Bible at home, the pastor reading in church, how difficult the Bible is to understand, how old it is, or what? Lead them into questions and comments about the Bible as a book.

Then discuss how the Bible is a gift. Do they agree with this? If so, in what ways is it a gift? *(It comes from God; it provides many truths we need.)* What are the key events in the Old and New Testaments? And of what importance are these events in our lives today?

As we learn more about the Bible and why it was written, we see that people wanted to learn from the things God was doing for them. They wanted to tell the story of how they had seen God in the experiences of their lives. Their story is our story also. The Bible comes alive when we see it as the story of God's continuous acts in the lives of people like us, for he still reveals himself in our lives, just as he did in these stories.

Write the words *divine* and *human* on the board. Why do we use these two words in studying the Bible? The chapter points out that the Bible is the record of God's choosing a people to be his own. But humans tell the story. Just as God uses humans now to tell his story, he used them in writing the Bible.

The diversity of the Bible. Have your students turn to their Bibles. Spend a minute or two looking at the list of contents which gives the names and order of the books. Does this look like other books they have read? What is different? Point out that there are many books within this book.

Take time to look at some of the different kinds of writing within the Bible. Assign pairs of students to look at the following passages:

Job 14	(poetry)	Exodus 20	(laws)
Psalm 84	(song)	Acts 2	(history)
Genesis 37	(story)	Isaiah 35	(prophecy)
Matthew 13	(parable)		

It isn't necessary to explain or analyze these passages. The point is to show the diversity of the Bible. It is a collection of books containing many types of writing with a central theme running throughout.

The theme of the Bible. The unifying theme of the Bible is that of God's grace, his love which never gives up on us. Ask your students how this love shows itself. Let them use their books to find sentences like: "It shows itself in the goodness of creation." (What are some examples of the goodness of creation?) "He kept coming back to try some new way to reach these people that he loved so much." (What are some ways in which he has tried to reach us?)

Together make a list of events and stories from the Bible that they can remember in which someone was in danger, sick, or in trouble, and God reached out to help. Our purpose is to emphasize that the Bible is the story of God and his love for his people. Write names and events on the board as the class members recall stories. If they need help, give them Bible references. Some that might be used are:

Noah and the ark	(Genesis 6-9)
David and Goliath	(1 Samuel 17)
Abraham and Isaac	(Genesis 22)
Daniel in the lions' den	(Daniel 6:16-28)
Joseph sold into slavery	(Genesis 37-41)
Jesus raising Lazarus	(John 11:38-44)
Jesus healing the paralytic	(Mark 2:1-11)
Peter rescued from prison	(Acts 12:1-11)

Why this is important to us. Save some time for reviewing the introductions that were made at the beginning of the hour. Ask how many think they know everyone in the class by name. Are there some they need to get better acquainted with? It is important for you to establish that the class is a *caring* group—that God loves each person in it and we have the opportunity to grow closer together each week.

You might point out how important it is that we learn to know each other. Just as our name is important to us and we respect people who know us by name, so others want to be known by name. Remind your class that you care about each of them and that God loves each of them. What he has to tell us in the Bible is the story of a new people—and it includes us!

Home assignment

It is important to tell the class what you expect them to have prepared for next week. Assign the reading of Chapter 2 in the student book. Encourage them to read carefully not only the chapter, but the Bible passages referred to in the chapter. And remind them that everyone should have a notebook in which to keep class notes and assignments.

Closing prayer

For this session, you could take the lead and offer a prayer thanking God for the opportunity to meet as a class and asking that God might help you in your study together.

Promises, Promises

Objective
The objective of this lesson is to develop the story of God's covenant with Abraham and Abraham's faith in the fulfillment of that covenant, and to explain how we are heirs of that promise, too.

Biblical basis
Genesis 12:1-3, 10-20; 15:1-6; 18:9-15; 22:1-14

Background information
It is important for you to be familiar with the story of Abraham. All Christians and Jews can look to Abraham as their spiritual father. We, too, are heirs of the covenant God made with Abraham.

The covenant or promise found in Gen. 12:1-3 was really threefold in nature. God promised (1) land, (2) a great nation, and (3) a blessing. The development of this covenant is the theme of the Old Testament and its ultimate fulfillment is found in the New Testament.

Remember that the land promised to Abraham goes by a number of names —the promised land, the holy land, Canaan, Israel, Palestine. Your class may be more familiar with some of these names than others—in future lessons you will want to make sure they know the place is the same even though the name changes.

Preparation for class
You will need at least two visual aids to help you illustrate this important lesson. One is the map of the Old Testament world found in both teacher and student books. It will help your class to trace the journey made by Abraham. The other visual aid needed is your own version of a family tree. On the chalkboard or on a piece of tagboard, make your family tree. Put at least three generations on it if you can.

Then study Genesis 12–24 to make sure you understand the story of Abraham, and carefully read Chapter 2 in the student book. In preparing this lesson, keep the idea of family in mind—the family of God to which we all belong.

The lesson experience
As your students arrive, use the time to get further acquainted with them, and encourage them to get to know each other. It might be wise to use name tags again, especially if you are having trouble with some of the names. Make it a point to use their names as you share together during the class discussion.

Begin with prayer. If you lead, give thanks that we are all descendants of Abraham and members of God's family. Thank God for the families we belong to, and his faithfulness in keeping his promises to us.

The family tree. Ask your students to take out the notebooks they will be using to write in throughout the course. The family tree can be one of their first entries. You will want to post the tree you have made of your family where everyone can see it. Explain how to construct such a tree, beginning with themselves, brothers, and sisters on the bottom, and building up to parents and grandparents. Give them a few minutes to draw this in their notebooks, then have a sharing time in which you talk about things like: How many generations can you trace back? Who do you think you resemble on your tree as to looks, personality, abilities? What's most important to you about your parents and grandparents?

Then ask: How long has your family been in this town? In this state? In this country? How would you like to have your family move to a strange place? What would you think about if your parents announced such a move?

All this serves as an introduction to the story of Abraham who left familiar surroundings and took his family to an unknown place.

Open your student books. Direct the class to Chapter 2 of the student book. It might be wise to give them a little time to skim the pages of this lesson, and to briefly review the Bible readings from Genesis. Some of your students will probably not have read the lesson. They should take this time to at least begin reading the story in the student book.

Look at the Old Testament map (on page 5 in this guide and on page 206 in the student book). Note where Mesopotamia was located. Point out the Fertile Crescent (so named for its shape). The Euphrates and Tigris rivers are important sources of water for this area. Evidently Abraham's people originally lived around Ur and moved to Haran and settled there. They were a nomadic people who stayed in that area so that good pastures could be found for their livestock. It was from Haran that God called Abraham and promised to do great things for him and his descendants.

Perhaps you could ask: What is it about this story that makes it important for us? Is it more than just ancient history? What was the relationship between God and Abraham? How is this relationship similar to the one between God and ourselves? The good news is that the promise of great things comes also to us.

Pay special attention to the word *covenant*. What words does your class use to explain *covenant*? Place them on the board. They will probably be words like *promise* . . . *agreement* . . . *deal* . . . *contract*. Which one do they think comes closest to what God's covenant with Abraham was like?

The promise idea really captures the biblical meaning behind covenant. God had already made a decision about Abraham—even before Abraham believed it. It was a unique kind of promise in that no matter what Abraham was like, or what he did, God would not change his mind.

Open your Bibles. As a group, read aloud Gen. 12:1-3 and 15:1-6. Underscore for your group the amazing agreement and the amazing response found in these passages:

1. God promised Abraham he would give him a land, a nation, and a blessing—no strings attached. He didn't say "as soon as you shape up" or "when you reach age 21." God loves us and accepts us as we are!

2. Abraham believed God! He responded in faith. He trusted God and did what God asked him to do, even though it seemed foolish at the time. God wants each of us to take him at his word!

Let your class talk for a brief while about the times they have received promises, particularly from their parents. What are some of the things they have been promised? Did they believe they would get these things? Why did they believe it or not believe it? Were there times when it meant a long time of waiting and trusting that the parents could really fulfill their promise? Was it easy to trust when it looked as if the promise wouldn't be fulfilled? What kinds of things stand in the way of parents fulfilling their promises to their families?

The challenges. Review Gen. 12:10-20 and 18:9-15. What is the first problem here that threatens the fulfillment of the promise God made to Abraham? What does Abraham do about it? The second problem Abraham meets has to do with his wife. What do you think of his idea? How would you have dealt with this problem? Note what happens to Abraham as a result of his deceit. Why did Sarah laugh? How does the whole matter turn out in the end? What does this tell us about God?

Ask your students to remember a time when they were in some kind of danger or trouble and acted in a way they know was wrong (lied or did something tricky to make things go their way). How did it turn out? Did their family know about this incident? Was there forgiveness? What can we learn from Abraham's problems and God's dealings with those problems that we might apply to our own failings?

Have someone read Gen. 22:1-14 aloud and then ask the students to write a sentence about how they would feel if they were Abraham and a sentence about how they would feel if they were Isaac. Then share some of the things that have been written. Have there been times when we didn't trust our parents, or didn't understand what they wanted us to do, or why they asked us to do something? All we know from the biblical account is that Abraham was faithful—he trusted God to do the impossible. And God did. What applications can we make from this for our lives?

Draw a picture or symbol. Have each student try to depict one of these stories of Abraham with a symbol. It need not be elaborate; they may draw a picture if they like, but encourage them to put their ideas into one visual image. They might take just one word—*promise* or *covenant* or *faith*—and draw a symbol for it. This should be done in the student notebook and if there is no time for sharing the symbols, use them next session as a review of the Abraham story.

Make a promise. Divide the class into teams of two. Have them think for a minute about something they would like to promise to do for the other person during the next week. Make it something special, but not costly or too difficult. Make it personal—something the partners would appreciate and that would be good for them. Have them write their partner's name and the promise in their notebooks, and ask them to try to fulfill that promise during the next week without the other person realizing what they are doing. They will report in class next week how they fulfilled their promise, and also how they felt about the promise made to them.

Then briefly look at the titles and subtitles in Chapter 3 and assign it for next time. Close with a brief prayer by you or a student.

In the Beginning

Objective
The objective of this lesson is to emphasize the goodness of God's creation and to point out our responsibility to use it properly.

Biblical basis
Genesis 1–2

Background information
Review in your mind your own understanding of the creation story. Do you view it as a scientific account of how the world began, or is it actually a religious story about God caring for his people? It might help in preparing for this lesson to review the course objectives listed in the introduction.

Our mission is *not* to present a strong argument for the creation occurring in six 24-hour days. We need plan no defense against the theories of the evolution of the world. Our emphasis here, as stated in the introduction, is helping the students to see the Bible as the story of God and his love for his people. The lesson should be planned keeping this in mind.

We are not in opposition to what our students have learned in school about the age and making of the earth. Rather, our story focuses on *who* and *why* rather than *when* and *how*. That is, who created and why did he create? Be prepared to work at this emphasis so that you don't get misled into a fruitless discussion on the theories concerning creation. Remember that this may be the first time your students have been presented with the idea that the biblical account is not meant to be scientific.

Preparation for class
By this time you should be acquainted with each pupil on a first-name basis. Encourage them to learn the names of all their classmates if they did not previously know them. Suggest they work with different people whenever you use small groups or partners. Emphasize that the class is a "caring" group, which means we accept each individual as a worthwhile person, a member of our family of faith. Help them to see themselves as God's chosen people, just as the biblical people were chosen and loved by him.

Make sure your notebook has attendance records to help you know when each person was present or absent, what projects the students have done and the progress they are making week by week.

By this time, everyone should be making weekly notebook entries. Each notebook will be different and should reflect what the lesson says to the individual student. You can help by suggesting certain things everyone should write down, such as chapter headings and the family tree we used in Chapter 2.

Encourage them to write notes as they work each week. When they read in their Bibles, a sentence or two about the passage will help them remember it. As they do their home assignments, a brief paragraph reviewing the chapter will remind them of main points.

The idea of the notebook is not only to give students something on paper about what they are doing in class, but to help make each lesson personal for them by having them write in their own words what they have read or talked about that week. You may want to collect the notebooks at periodic intervals—not with the idea of correcting them, but rather to see how each student is viewing the course. You will also gain some new insights into that student.

If there is time, you might have the class work together on a banner about creation and our responsibility for it. Or have them gather a series of pictures for a collage. In either project, you simply need some materials such as felt, burlap, or fabric for a banner, or poster board and magazines for a collage, in addition to scissors and glue.

The lesson experience

As the class begins, briefly review the first two chapters. Point out that Abraham is the person we began with as the founder of faith. Ask them to recall how he was called by God and his response. What promises did God make to Abraham? How did Abraham respond? Have they kept this information in their notebooks?

Remind your students of the promise they made to someone in the class last week. Did they keep the promise? Ask for a few to relate their promises and their successes and failures in regard to it. Then allow some students to relate how they felt about someone "owing" them something because of a promise. Were they looking for "signs" from that person? Did they know or guess what the promise was? How did they feel as they waited? Try to draw some comparisons between the promises we make to one another and those God makes to us. For us, the point of Abraham's story is that God keeps his promises, even in the midst of our questioning and impatience.

Then make the transition to the creation chapter by simply saying that although we look at Abraham as the beginning of God's people, we know there were people before him. Naturally we have questions about them, too. Our chapter this week deals with questions about where the people before Abraham came from and what God thought of them. Now is a good time for a prayer, asking God to bless our study.

Open your books. Take a few minutes for the students to review the three main questions asked in this chapter and the answers given. Write them on the board as you review them and encourage your students to write their answers in their notebooks.

1. Who is responsible for this world?
2. Is it good?
3. What do we do with it?

Spend some time discussing the answers to these questions. Reread Genesis 1 and 2. Who was responsible for creating everything in the world? Ask them to count how many times the word *good* is used. What does this tell them about how God created the world? The world is not accidental—it was his intention and purpose to make all things, and what he made was good!

This is where comments and questions about how the world came into being will come up. Remember that we are concerned with the *who* of creation and not the *how*. We are interested in God who made it happen! We see in the Bible that he made all things good, and that there was purpose in all that he created.

Furthermore, there is something special about each one of us. Open your Bibles to Gen. 1:26-30. Have someone read this passage aloud. What does it mean to be created in God's "image"? Write the word on the board and try to define it. Remind the students of the family tree we drew in our notebooks. Who in the family are we like? Do we look like God or is the likeness in other areas? Make sure they get the idea that human beings can relate to God in a way different from any other creature. Then move from the idea of the special status people enjoy as the height of God's creation to the special responsibility that goes with it.

What do your students think it means to have dominion over something? What does this phrase have to do with responsibility? Ask each one to write a few words in his or her notebook about the phrase. Then ask them to share in twos or threes what they think our job is in keeping the creation as God intended it to be. Select one from each group to report and list the things we should be doing. You'll want the list to include things like:

- using the plants and animals for food
- keeping the water pure for drinking

- enjoying the creation (beauty, recreation, housing)
- controlling the environment
- making a living off the land

Some of these may be difficult to see today in our sophisticated society, but discuss about how well we have fulfilled this responsibility. Have we done a good job in taking care of the world entrusted to us?

Review with your class the three problems relating to creation suggested in the chapter: ecology, overpopulation, and the importance of women. Remind them that the Bible is primarily concerned with religious questions about who God is and what he thinks of us. When we are confronted with questions about why disease and disaster are around, it's good to remind ourselves that we have been given dominion and that we have a responsibility to use it to keep the creation working well. Ask these questions:

1. Who is responsible for land-use? Supplying drinking water? Highway construction? Garbage disposal? What do these things have to do with us?

2. If God says in Gen. 1:28 that man should be fruitful and multiply, why do we need population control? What are our responsibilities here?

3. Are both man and woman created in God's image? Is one of more importance than the other?

The purpose of these questions is to relate God's creation plan to our day. We too are created by God, able to have a unique relationship with him, and responsible for our world. But something went wrong with this perfect creation. We study this in the next lesson.

Creation project. Now is the time to spend some minutes together thinking and sharing. Let the students decide what they want to put on their banner or collage and whether they want to make one large one together or individual ones. Each item included, whether picture, word, or symbol, should have a reason for being there. What do we want to say about the creation with this project?

Put them to work as soon as their ideas begin to form. Try to involve the whole class as much as possible, reviewing the ideas of the chapter and asking them for their personal feelings about what the lesson has to say. What message about creation does their project convey?

Closing prayer

Ask for a volunteer for closing prayer. Suggest a few ideas that might be included about the world God made and our own responsibility to take care of it. This might encourage someone who is not sure what to say. At the same time you might ask for a volunteer to offer prayer next week. You can suggest that prayers need not be written out or formal, but are meant to be a sharing with the class. As the students get to know one another and feel comfortable, praying together will become more spontaneous and personal. The best encouragement is a regular practice of prayer and an accepting attitude toward all contributors.

Home assignment

Encourage your students to read Chapter 4 early in the week. This will give them the background for their home assignment. They are to record in their notebooks two or three instances in which they had to make a choice involving right or wrong. Did they feel good or bad? Did they do something that hurt or helped someone? Did others find out? If they were doing something wrong, did they get caught—feel guilty—make excuses? The purpose is to show that God has given each of us the power to choose. We are not mechanical robots.

Trouble in the Garden

Objective
The objective of this lesson is to show the results of sin in the world God created, but also to point out God's continuing love and promises to us.

Biblical basis
Genesis 3:1—11:9

Background information
As we look at this lesson, it's important to remember that the accounts in Genesis 3–11 are not meant to be scientific history, but their purpose is to show us the results of disobedience. What went wrong in the Garden of Eden? Who was responsible for the trouble? What happened because of it?

We see that sin separates people from their creator and that God allows us to choose evil, even when he knows what will happen. We also look at other results of sin, particularly guilt, jealousy, murder, pride, and other continuing problems. Try to plan the lesson so that there is a balance between the biblical story of the fall into sin and what this means for us today.

Preparation for class
Read Chapter 4 and the chapters in Genesis. This is a rather long section, so plan to skim over parts of it. This section shows the results of wrong choices and our tendency to excuse ourselves when we do wrong.

Examine "The Great Game of Life" (see page 17). This is meant to help the class identify problems and consequences involved in choices we make in life. Do not spend the entire class period on the game, but use it to get into the biblical account of the fall and the resulting problems. Also, help your students remember this is just a game. Real life is much more complex.

The lesson experience
One way to begin the period is with "The Great Game of Life." It will get everyone interested in the idea of choosing and making decisions, and is a natural way to lead into the stories of the fall, the flood, and the Tower of Babel. Have all the materials ready when your class arrives, and immediately after attendance is taken, explain the game rules. Lay the game out on your desk or a small table. Make sure everyone knows what is happening, and let the game be fun! Play for about 15 minutes or until a winner finishes the course.

Be careful about making too many comparisons between the game and real-life decisions. Be sure to point out that the choices we make are often more gray than black and white, and often the consequences of a good decision can be mixed too. We can do something unkind and have it turn out well or make an attempt to do a good thing and have it turn out poorly. The idea of the game is simply to open thought and discussion about the nature of choices and decisions.

You can explore with your class how they felt about the Choice cards and the shortcuts—did they venture on them or were the chances of going back too high? Did they feel the decisions and consequences were fair or unfair? How did they feel about landing on a space that made them wait? All of these are questions which can be used again when we look at our Bible story and see what happened to that perfect creation God planned.

Take time for prayer. At this point, prayer can be a bridge in moving from the game to the lesson. A student was to be prepared with a prayer this week. After the prayer, take a minute to remind the class that this kind of sharing brings us together as a family in faith and makes us aware of God's presence. Ask now for a volunteer for next week. Suggest that something from next week's lesson be used as the theme of the prayer. Perhaps it would be helpful to talk a bit about prayer as conversation.

Look at the lesson. Spend a few minutes reviewing this week's lesson. Then place these two questions on the board: "Who caused the trouble?" and "Who has the answer?"

Ask them to retell in their own words what they think went wrong in the Garden of Eden. Listen carefully to what they are saying. Whom are they blaming? Use their answers as a starting point for these other questions about the decision to disobey God:

1. Whose fault is it that the world changed from what God created?
2. Why did God give us this freedom of choice?
3. Who is the snake? What part does the snake play in the story?
4. Who suffers as a result of this disobedience? What evidence of fear and shame do we find in Chapter 3?

Use the notebooks. Ask the class to use their notebooks. Under the heading "Who caused the trouble?" suggest they summarize in a few sentences the main ideas of this story: Adam and Eve had freedom; they chose to disobey God; the snake is the tempter and bears guilt too; both man and woman disobey and both are punished; the results are many: fear, shame, guilt, blaming others, hiding from God, loss of the garden.

Then briefly review the three additional examples of how bad conditions became as a result of evil in the world. Can they name some specific evils from the story of Cain and Abel? Can they see a pattern of evil developing in these various incidents? Why did God send the flood? Why was Noah chosen to build the ark? Try to imagine how he felt about carrying out God's orders to build the ark. In what ways are our lives like the Tower of Babel story? (We too may try to get along without God, and often end up frustrated.)

Then discuss the second question, "Who has the answer?" Review the answers given in the student book. What glimmers of hope are found after each of the three disasters? Have them write this second question in their notebooks and briefly summarize their answers.

Review the covenant between God and Abraham that we studied in Chapter 2. Remember Abraham's faith: he trusted God's promise concerning a land, a son, and a blessing. You might want to look at Gen. 12:1-3 and 15:1-6 again.

God continues to care about what happens to us in spite of our wrongdoing and our disobedience. He loves us. God is steadfast. That's the happy ending to this biblical account of the trouble in the garden and its results.

While their notebooks are still open, ask your students to share with each other the kinds of things they recorded during the week about choices. They were to write two or three instances in which they had choices to make involving right or wrong, and to record the results of those choices.

Encourage this sharing. It may not be easy for students to talk about things that are of importance to them. Assure them that we all make choices and face results. Remind them of the game we played earlier. Did any of them make those kinds of decisions this past week? Were they involved in any decisions about sharing, cheating, gossiping, being kind, giving of themselves, helping others? How did they make these decisions? What happened as a result?

The purpose of this discussion is to point out that all of us have the freedom of choosing, and we don't always decide to do what's right. Help them to see that we are involved with the same problems that came into the world as a result of the disobedience in the garden. Can they make some comparisons

Turn to page 23

Game directions

"The Great Game of Life" gives your class a chance to see how often they are confronted with choices. Some are much more important than others, and we often react without thinking to a number of choices presented to us. Use the playing board printed in this guide or reproduce it on poster board for a bigger game area. Bring dice and playing markers to class. If your class is small, each student may take a turn throwing and moving around the board. If the class is large, divide into two teams and let team members alternate moving.

Everyone begins on the space marked *start*. The player rolls one of the dice and moves his marker the number of spaces shown and then waits his next turn unless the space he lands on contains some consequences. He must do as this space directs and then wait his next turn.

The Choice cards are drawn only by those landing on spaces marked *"Take a Choice."* Then the player must do as the card states—these should be read out loud for the whole class to hear. There are three short routes to the home base, but note that they are not always convenient ways! The short routes can only be taken by those landing directly on the space which says they may take it. The first player or team *Home* wins the game.

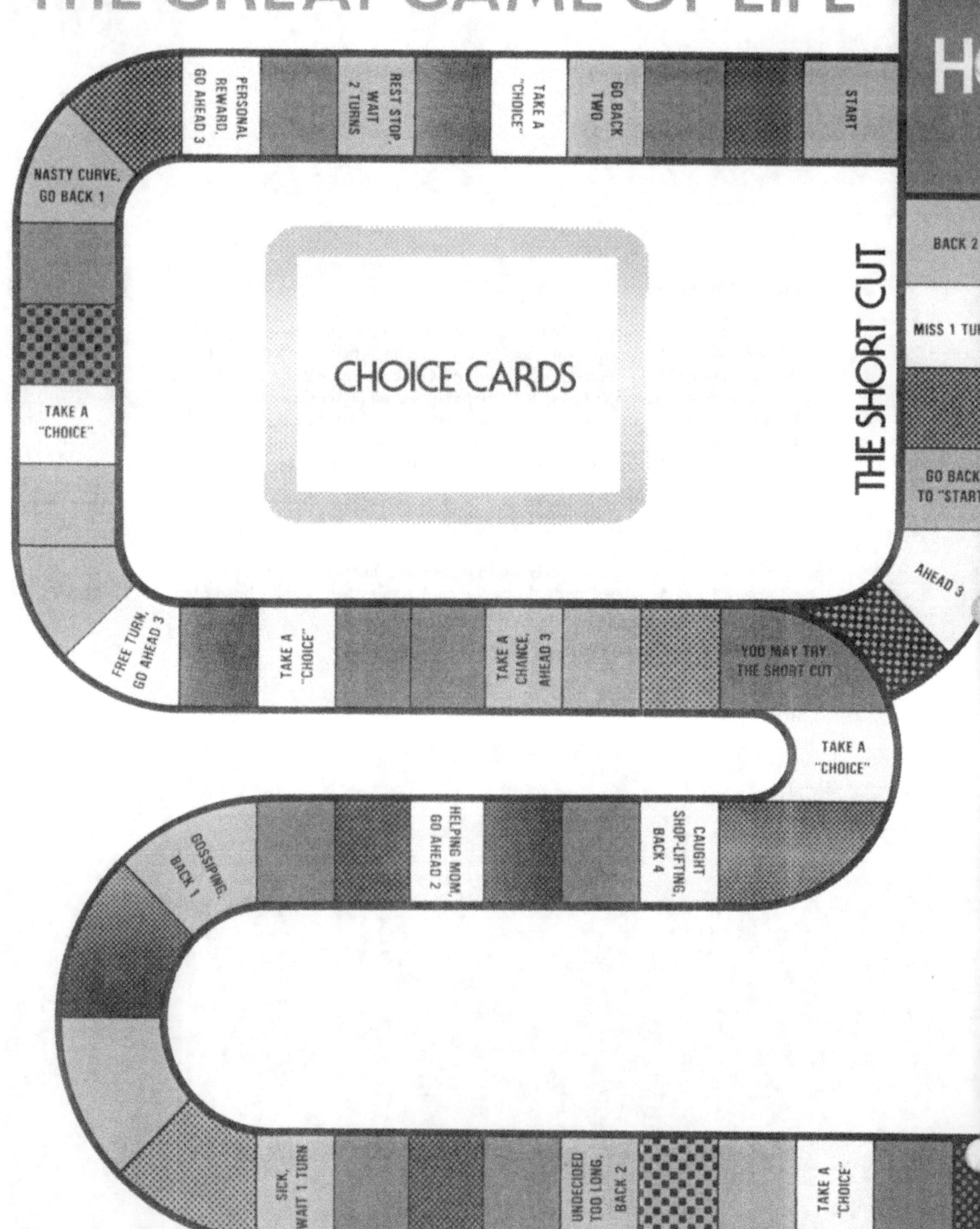

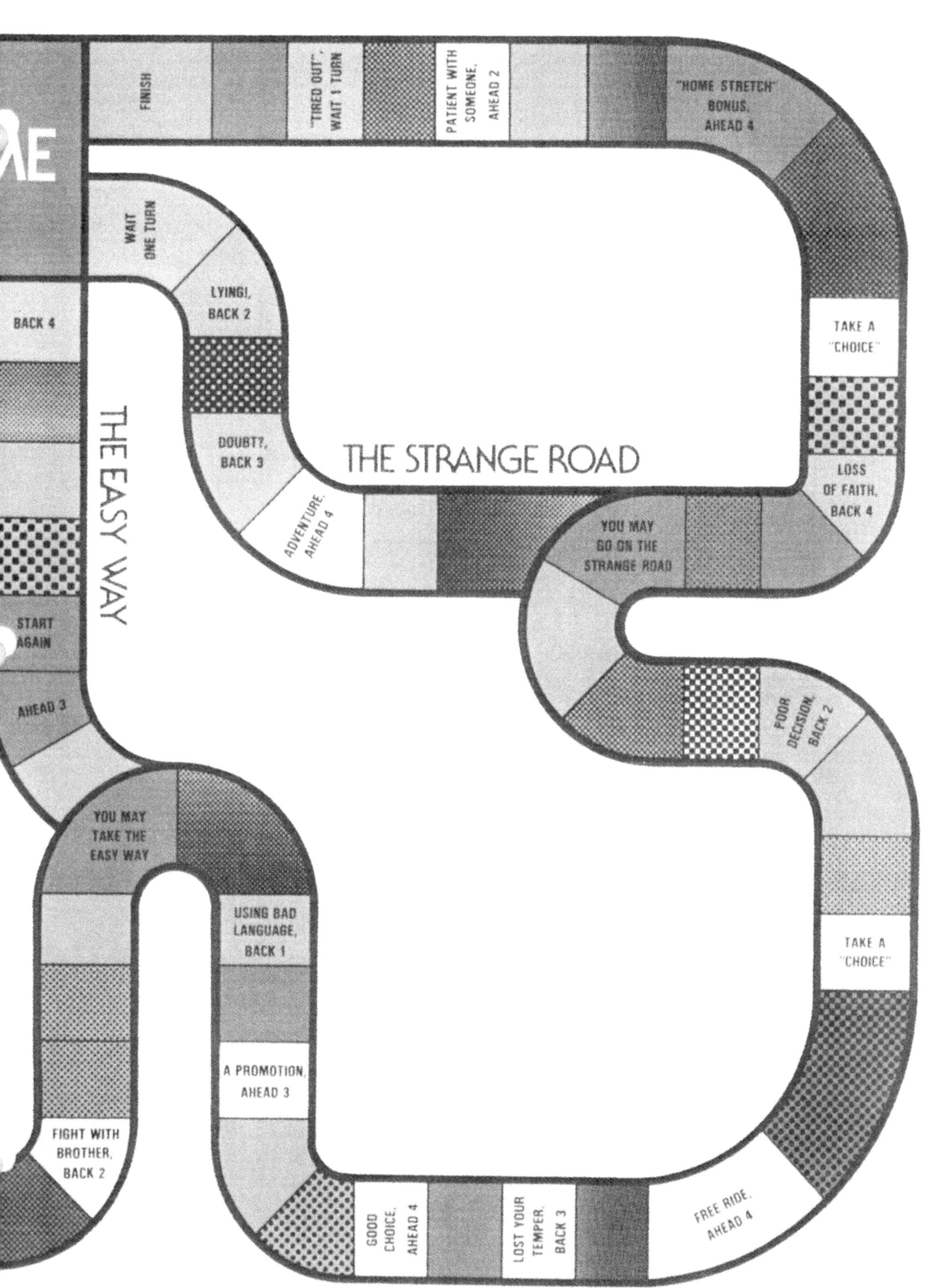

You let your mom know you liked her dinner. **Go AHEAD 3 spaces**	**You skipped school to go bowling downtown.** **Go BACK 1 space**	**You refused to give a friend the answers to a test you had taken.** **Go AHEAD 2 spaces**
You repeated some gossip about a classmate. **Go BACK 2 spaces**	**You listened to a friend's problems, even though you have plenty of your own.** **Go AHEAD 4 spaces**	**You cheated in a game of touch football.** **Go BACK 3 spaces**
You ate lunch with a new girl in school. **Go AHEAD 4 spaces**	**You made fun of a boy who tripped in gym class.** **Go BACK 4 spaces**	**You helped your little brother with his math.** **Go AHEAD 2 spaces**
You kept silent when you heard friends talking about that "stupid" boy. **Go BACK 1 space**	**You didn't take part in teasing the girl who is so shy.** **Go AHEAD 4 spaces**	**The gang you were with shoplifted a radio and you helped.** **Go BACK 4 spaces**
You decided to spend part of Saturday collecting trash along the street. **Go AHEAD 3 spaces**	**You lied to your father when he asked you about your school work.** **Go BACK 2 spaces**	**You didn't try the pills that everyone says help you to think better.** **Go AHEAD 4 spaces**
You put someone down in order to make a new friend admire you. **Go BACK 3 spaces**	**You caught a ride home when the party punch turned out to be beer.** **Go AHEAD 2 spaces**	**You took time to clean your room before going out with your friends.** **Go AHEAD 2 spaces**

CHOICE CARD	CHOICE CARD	CHOICE CARD
CHOICE CARD	CHOICE CARD	CHOICE CARD
CHOICE CARD	CHOICE CARD	CHOICE CARD
CHOICE CARD	CHOICE CARD	CHOICE CARD
CHOICE CARD	CHOICE CARD	CHOICE CARD
CHOICE CARD	CHOICE CARD	CHOICE CARD

Continued from page 16

between themselves and the Bible characters being studied in this lesson? Do they make some of the same mistakes and feel fear, guilt, and shame, and hide from what they know is right?

We are caught in the same problems that humans have faced for centuries. Is there any hope? The answer is a resounding "YES!" God enters where we least expect him, lends his presence in the midst of a world going in the wrong direction, and fulfills promises to his people in spite of their problems.

The end of the story has to do with faith. That's the end of our story too. We can believe that God forgives us and loves us—that is what faith is all about. We are responsible for the condition of our world, but the same God who created it still loves us and will not leave us without help. He took care of Adam and Eve, he looked after Abraham and saved Noah, and he surrounds us with his love, too. We can count on him.

To illustrate this, you might use the idea of a family. This is usually a relationship which holds us even when we do wrong. Ask your students who it is that helps them out when they are in trouble. Even though parents or brothers and sisters get angry with us, we can usually depend on them when we need them. We belong to them! They feel a responsibility for us. If we do something wrong, they correct us, discipline us, and may even punish us; but they do not desert us. In some of the same ways, God looks after us as a loving father. We are his creation and even though we separate ourselves from him by disobeying, he still loves us.

Home assignment

Ask your class to read Chapter 5 of the student book for next week. Remind them that these stories are our history, too, because they tell us how God worked with and related to the people that came before us. They should carefully do the Bible reading that is mentioned in the chapter because this is where the story is really written. This is where God tells us how he plans and promises great things for us.

Tracing the Promise

Objective

The objective of this lesson is to show how God's promise to Abraham continued to be given to his descendants.

Biblical basis

Genesis 16; 21:8-21; 25:19-28; 27:1-45; 30:1-24; 50:15-21

Background information

We want to present this lesson as personal and exciting history, for these Bible stories have to do with our heritage. They tell stories about a particular people and their relationships with each other and with God. These were real people with real problems, and God continued to love and care for them even when things seemed nearly hopeless.

The concept of *selection* is important here. Spend some time thinking about what it means to be *chosen* by God. Why does God choose some people and not others? Why doesn't he pick better examples for us rather than people who seem to make so many mistakes? What is it we are actually chosen to do?

Carefully read the material in the reading book and the corresponding chapters in the Bible. You'll notice that God manages to bring good out of human evil. For instance, Joseph's life worked out quite differently than his brothers intended. Also, God promised to make a nation of Ishmael after Sarah asked Abraham to cast him out with his mother, Hagar. Many times we see that God's people cause a derailment of his promises to them. Nevertheless, he stays with them and often uses their very mistakes for his purposes.

Make this session as personal as possible. Focus on the people in the stories as real people who had hopes and dreams just as we have. They took chances and tried to work out plans for their lives. They did wrong, made errors, and were not perfect, but God loved them just as he loves us. Allow the Bible characters to be human. That's the secret of making Bible characters alive for young people reading about them centuries later.

Preparation for class

A Bible commentary will be helpful in giving additional information about some of these characters. What can you learn about Hagar and Ishmael and the growth of the Arab nations? How does the tension between Hagar and Sarah relate to modern conflicts between Arabs and Jews? What was Egypt like and what happened to Joseph in Egypt?

You might want to use the family tree again, connecting the idea of our own family with the family tree of these ancient people who belong to our family of faith.

Copy this family tree of Abraham on a poster or on the chalkboard:

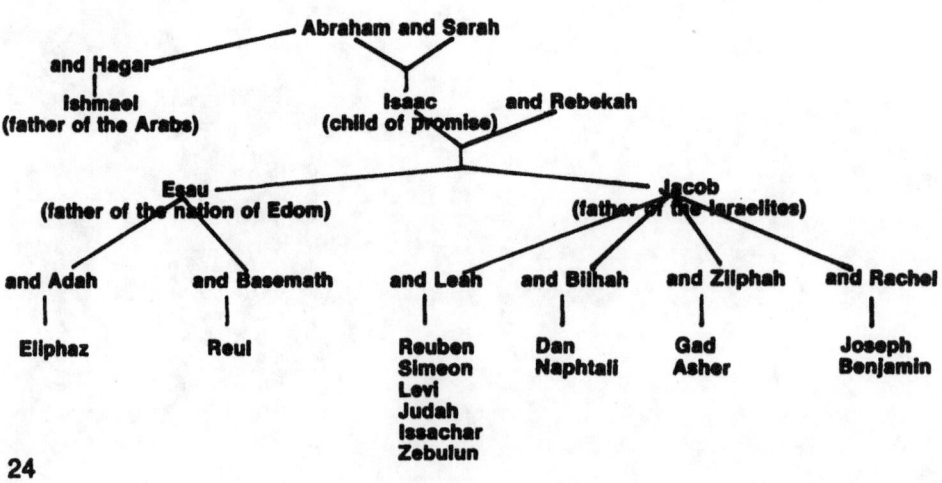

This diagram will be ready to use in class when you talk about the people who are chosen and others who are excluded. Outline or trace in red the children who become the next generation through whom God's promise continues. Remember that God loves all people, but part of the lesson experience should deal with the question of why he uses certain people and not others.

Isaac was chosen over Ishmael because Ishmael was the son of a slave woman, Hagar. Although Esau was the older son and the likely candidate for the birthright, God had told Rebekah that the elder would serve the younger (Gen. 25:23). Then in the third generation we find that Joseph is the firstborn son of Jacob's favorite wife, Rachel.

The lesson experience

Get the session started on a lively note with a quick quiz. Pick out your own 10 questions from the four previous chapters, or use the following. Either write these questions on a large piece of poster board or have them mimeographed. Ask for short answers. Give your class five minutes to write the answers and then quickly check the quiz.

1. The Bible is the story of _____ *(God and his people)*.
2. Name two kinds of writing we find in the Bible *(poetry, parables, history, songs, stories, laws, prophecies)*.
3. Write a phrase that you feel is the theme of the Bible *(God loves us)*.
4. What is a covenant? *(an agreement, promise, deal, contract)*.
5. What did God promise Abraham? *(a land, a nation, and a blessing)*.
6. What did Abraham have to do to receive the promise? *(nothing)*.
7. Was the world created in six days or did it evolve over many centuries? *(the Bible isn't meant to answer scientific questions, but to reveal God's love)*.
8. Whose responsibility is it to take care of God's creation? *(people's, mine)*.
9. What went wrong with God's great creation? *(people disobeyed God)*.
10. How do we know God still loved his people after they disobeyed him? *(he still cared for Adam and Eve; he made promises to Abraham and fulfilled them; he saved Noah; he sent the rainbow, etc.)*.

Do not be rigid in demanding answers. Instead look for answers that get the basic idea. Briefly discuss the answers, but don't get hung up on technicalities. Sometimes students worry about getting everything exactly right and argue over trivial differences. Have students correct their own papers so they can quickly see their mistakes. Collect the papers so you can review them later. Suggest that this kind of quiz reviews the main points of past lessons.

Look at the chapter. Ask your students to open their reading books and review Chapter 5. While they're doing this, post your family tree of Abraham's descendants and take attendance.

Are you getting to know these young people? Keep in mind what they look like, whom they like to be with, whether they come together or alone, who is absent and why, their interests, and anything else that will help you in understanding them. There is little learning without relationships. You must get to know your students as individuals in order to grow together during this time. While they review their home assignments, notice who it is that is reviewing, who is reading for the first time, and who is completely disinterested. These are clues to help you in teaching.

Discuss how the promise continues. Begin by asking, Who likes history? What is their favorite subject: math, science, English, Spanish? What about history? What kind of history do they remember studying? What things make history dull or uninteresting? What things make it exciting and personal? What famous people were fun to learn about?

The session this week concerns our family of faith. Abraham was the founder. His descendants are important because they reveal how God kept his promises after Abraham was dead.

These people have much in common with other historical people—they were very *real* people who did unusual things. Many were wrong at times and hard to deal with; they did things that changed life for their families and for us. And they are a lot like us—they made mistakes, had good and bad times, laughed and cried, loved and married, and were in and out of trouble.

Point out Abraham on the chart, mentioning that his child by the slave woman, Hagar, was not the child promised to Abraham through Sarah. Isaac was the long-awaited child of promise. Ishmael and Hagar were thrown out into the desert because of the jealousy of Sarah after Isaac was finally born. God promised that Ishmael would be the father of a great nation, though, and his descendants are today's Arab nations. Ask the class about the relationship between Arabs and Jews today. Notice how long-standing that feud has been!

Have a class member reread Gen. 25:19-28 aloud. Note that the Bible traces the story through Isaac, not Ishmael. The writers are Hebrews, not Arabs. Using the chart, move on to Isaac and his two sons, Esau and Jacob. Say something about the usual custom in those days concerning the birthright. Remember that the birthright determined who would head the next generation of the family. You may want to investigate the word *birthright* in a Bible dictionary. Esau should have been the chosen son but in Gen. 25:23 God tells Rebekah that the younger son will be served by the elder. This is a reminder that God does the choosing.

Jacob was a real trickster. He tricked his brother and his father into giving him the birthright. But Jacob became the father of all the Israelites (another name for God's chosen people). Later his name was changed to Israel. Esau became father of the nation of Edom (which means red), a small kingdom later dominated for years by Israel. So God's promise to Rebekah did come true. Even the tricky deeds of Jacob were used by God for good. In Genesis we see Jacob changing from a trickster to God's follower, but he's always interesting and very human.

The third generation involves Jacob's sons, who became the 12 tribes of Israel. Just as there were 12 tribes in the Old Testament, so Jesus chose 12 disciples in the New Testament. Since they had no king, these tribes became the organized government for the Israelites.

Remember that Jacob had 12 sons by four different wives. Two of the wives were Rachel and Leah, who were sisters. Remember the story of how Jacob was tricked into working extra years to obtain Rachel as his wife? Rachel was the favorite wife. The sons born to the maidservants, Zilpah and Bilhah, had a less favored status. We read much about Joseph in the Bible because he was the firstborn son of Jacob's favorite wife and had an important role in God's continuing promise of a nation and a blessing.

Note Joseph on the chart. Most of the last chapters in Genesis are about him and his people in Egypt. It was an unlikely location for people who had been promised a land of their own. How was God going to fulfill his promises?

What does it mean to be chosen? Write these questions on the board and suggest that your students write them in their notebooks:
1. How does God choose his people?
2. Why does God choose some and not others?
3. What is expected of those he chooses?

Talk about these questions one at a time, using the characters from the stories as a starting point. Why did God choose Abraham, or tricky Jacob, or any of the others? The point is that he chooses us, not because we deserve it, but because he loves us! God loved Jacob, even though he lied to his father! He loves us that way too!

Why does God choose some and not others? There is no easy answer. It is essential to keep in mind that God loves all the people he has made. But he set apart the Israelites as a special group to bring to all the world his message of love.

We, too, are chosen and given special responsibility. God has work for us to do as his people—life may be harder, not easier, because of that work. He chooses us not to relax and forget others, but to serve others.

There are many instances in the Bible of how God is able to work good out of the evil acts committed by his people. Each of us can think of times we've done something wrong and it worked out for good in spite of our selfish ways. God not only sticks with us when we disappoint him, he turns things around to make good come out of them! He knows we make mistakes. He stuck with Jacob and others when they did wrong things. He promises to do the same for us. God is in charge no matter what! He expects us to keep his promises in mind and to remember we are his even when times turn bad.

Closing prayer

End this class session with the student prayer that was assigned last week. Is there a volunteer for next week? Suggest that soon it might be time to begin sharing voluntarily in sentence prayers in class. Some classes may be ready for this already.

Home assignment

Ask your students to read Chapter 6 in the reading book and to be sure also to do the Bible reading. Assign each student to ask two people during the week who Moses was and to write the answer in his or her notebook. If there is time, skim through Chapter 6, highlighting a few of the interesting aspects of the chapter.

The Great Escape

Objective

The objective of this lesson is to present God as one who keeps his promises in spite of difficulties. He is a God of compassion for the weak, the helpless, and the oppressed, who sends a deliverer in the midst of our need.

Biblical basis

Exodus 2:1—3:20; 12:21-42; 14:1-30

Background information

The lesson centers on Moses, a great leader whom God sent to deliver his people in their need. We shall study three distinct 40-year periods in the life of Moses.

The story of Moses and the exodus is a familiar one. Some of your students may have seen films about Moses and the exodus. The main theme of this chapter, however, deals not so much with familiar events, but with the kind of God who made these events possible! Our emphasis in this lesson is the continuing promises God makes and keeps with his people, his great compassion for those who suffer, and the fact that he does send a deliverer. It might help to keep in mind that we are not so much emphasizing *how* the exodus came about, but *why* God sent Moses and what it meant to his people to be delivered.

Forty is a number which occurs again and again in the Bible. Note the use of the number 40 in the Noah story (Gen. 7:4, 12) and in the story of Jesus' temptation (Luke 4:1-3). It seems to be a number of special significance to the biblical writers. We cannot be sure that it means there were 40 actual years of Moses' life in each of these three periods. It might help to point out that this number 40 may mean a generation. The main point is that there are three definite divisions of time in the life of Moses. This is another one of those places where we find that the Bible is not concerned about exact details. The important thing is the story that tells about God and what he does for his people.

Preparation for class

Why not show a film or filmstrip about Moses which emphasizes how God used him as a great leader and deliverer at this time in history? Arrange to have it shown at the appropriate time in the class hour and then move to the biblical narrative. Preview the film so you can introduce it with a few questions to help your class view it with greater profit. An alternative would be to use the questions following the film as a way of leading into the Bible story.

The lesson experience

Begin the class by asking for a report on the interviews about Moses. Let students use their notebooks to share ideas that people gave them about Moses. What did people remember about him? On the board, list some of these things. When everyone has shared, encourage the class to add their own ideas to those you already have on the board. Some of the items may refer to what the chapter talks about as the three main divisions in the life of Moses. Point out that these are the matters we are interested in looking into more fully. Then lead into the idea that we also will talk about the three things that this story tells us about God. Can they remember them from Chapter 6?

With this brief introduction, it might be a good time to open the reading books and briefly review Chapter 6. Look for the three things this story tells us about God.

The film or filmstrip. This is a good time to use the audiovisual on Moses and the exodus. Use questions at either the beginning or end to stimulate good listening and viewing. You might take a minute to let the students know that

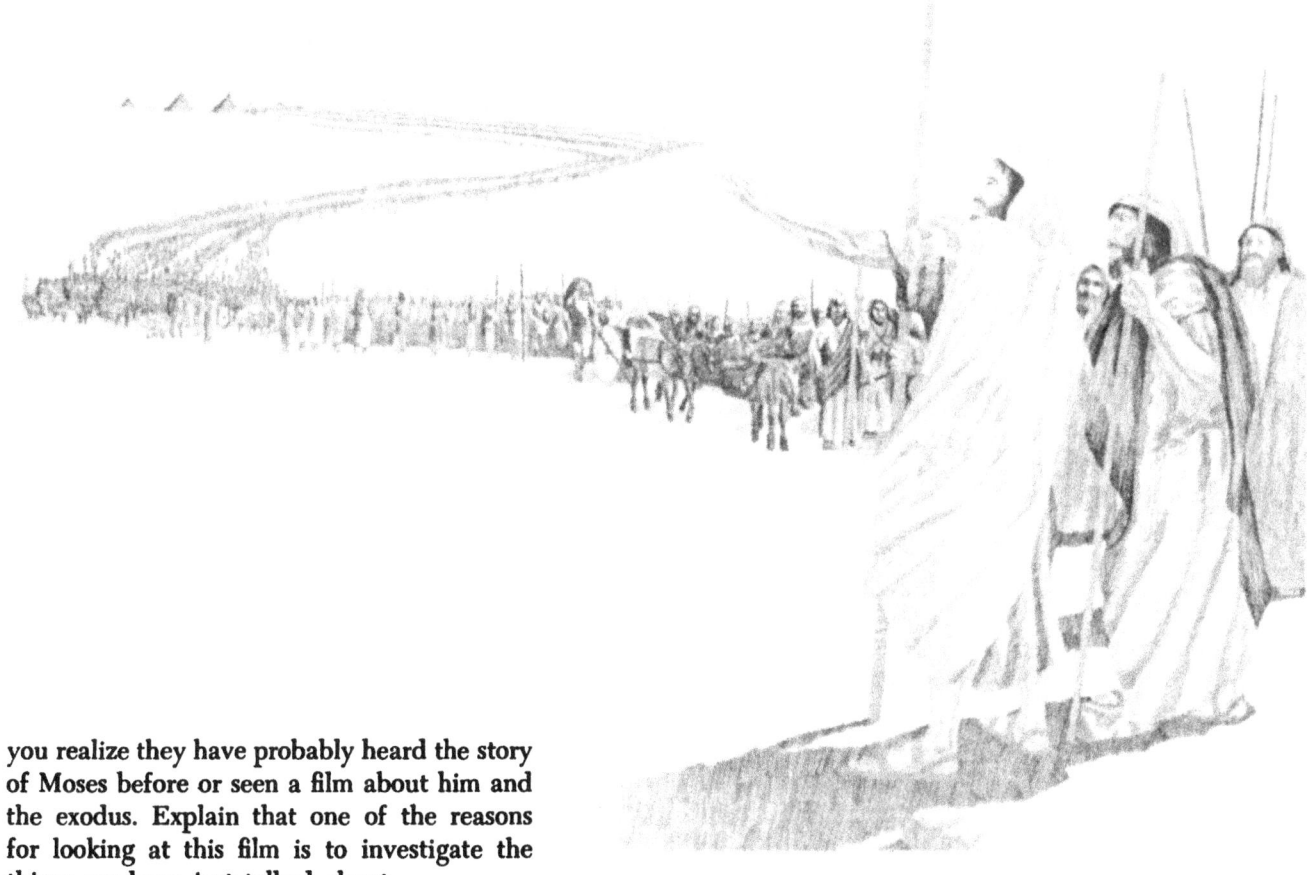

you realize they have probably heard the story of Moses before or seen a film about him and the exodus. Explain that one of the reasons for looking at this film is to investigate the things we have just talked about.

After the showing, remind the class of the chapter's main points about God and Moses. What did they feel the film was trying to convey? Did they pick up the ideas that the chapter was emphasizing? What incidents were most exciting to them? Could they remember significant divisions of time for Moses' life in the film? What seemed to mark these divisions? What was Moses like in the film? Use these questions and any others you have to lead into the actual study of the Bible story about Moses.

A mural or triptych. Divide the class into three sections, giving each section one of the assigned passages from Exodus.
  1. Exod. 2:1-15   Egypt
  2. Exod. 2:16—3:20   Wilderness
  3. Exod. 12:21-42; 14:1-30   Liberation

Ask each section to make notes while they read about the story. Then they should decide how they might depict in a drawing this period of Moses' life. Each section should settle on one idea or event to represent that period.

Provide large sheets of drawing paper or one continuous roll of shelf paper or three sheets of poster board for the class to use in this project. Encourage them to draw even if they feel they are not good at it. Bring crayons, pencils, chalk, and magic markers to help them complete the mural. Allow enough time for good work and then put the three parts together. Ask each group to choose a speaker to explain how they decided what to draw. Arrange the project for display after taping the sections into a three-piece unit. Use a prominent place, preferably in the narthex of your church, to display the drawings. Include a brief explanation.

Use of notebooks. After the project about Moses is completed, you may want to talk briefly with the class about the chapter again. Have them open their notebooks to make notes of important things that are said. First let them write down the three main divisions of Moses' life as they have just depicted it. Then review what this story says about God:

1. He keeps his promises—when he says something, he sticks to it.
2. He has compassion for those who are hurting.
3. God sends a leader or deliverer when his people need one.

You will probably have other ideas from the reading book, the film, and the class discussion that you want to have included in student notebooks. Add whatever you feel will be helpful to them.

How about us? Take some time for relating the learning in the lesson to everyday life. Why is it important for us to learn about the God of the Old Testament? What do we care if he keeps his promises? How might it affect us to believe that God has compassion for the weak, the downtrodden, the helpless? Do we believe God sends powerful leaders when people really need them? Can we think of any modern leaders who might be of this type? The God of the Hebrews is the same God we believe in—he cares about his people and he does something about it.

Closing prayer

If there is time, perhaps two or three students could offer a sentence prayer of their own, keeping in mind the lesson they've just studied and what they have learned about God. If time is short, you could lead in a prayer summarizing the main ideas of the lesson.

Home assignment

Ask your students to read Chapter 7 about law. Encourage them to do the Bible reading that is listed with the chapter. Next week's lesson is about Moses as a lawgiver. They should spend some time before then thinking of different types of laws to which they are subject. Ask them to make a short list of these laws in their notebooks. These lists will be used in next week's lesson.

7
You Shall Not

Objective
The objective of this lesson is to help the students see the law as something God gave us as a gift to help us live in the world he created. However, we do not qualify for God's love by obeying him. He loves us as we are.

Biblical basis
Exodus 20:1-17; 21:22-36; Leviticus 11:1-47

Background information
When we get to talking about laws, most young people tighten up because they are always hearing about what other people want them to do! They often feel that the whole world is made up of individuals and groups making laws to restrict and inhibit them, telling them what they are supposed to do and not do. They often tire of following rules set up by other people and wish to have a chance to make their own rules. They are most familiar with the negatives of the law: you should *not* do this or that. Not enough emphasis is placed on *who* made the laws and *why*.

One of the things we want most to happen in this class is for the students to begin to see that God loves us and that he gives us the law as a gift because he wants things to go well for us. The law is really for our own good. Help your class to see that keeping the law is not the way we qualify for God's special help or love, but rather it's our way of responding to the love he has already showered on us as a free gift.

There are different kinds of laws in the Bible, just as there are in our society today. Some of them change from time to time, depending on the particular needs of the times. But one thing remains constant—the law is a help for us in learning how to live in a good and loving relationship with God and with other people.

Preparation for class
This lesson covers much material. Pick activities that work best for your class. Include a review of the reading book chapter. Then prepare whatever activities you think are best for your class. You will find it helpful if you can plan field trips for a day or time other than your regular class time. Cover the biblical material first and use it as a foundation for outside experience.

Plan a panel or a field trip. The nature of law and its enforcement is a wide and interesting topic. You could invite a panel of people who deal with laws to come to your class to discuss questions about who makes laws and how they are kept, changed, and enforced. The panel might include a lawyer, city council member, judge, school principal, legislator, sheriff or policewoman, rabbi, pastor, parent, social worker, club president, etc. If you cannot get a number of people, select one person who is articulate about the law and its application and who also can be a positive witness to the need for law and its place in our world.

If you feel a field trip would be helpful, look around your community for places or people to visit that would help to better understand the law. It could be a city council meeting, a jail, a court hearing, a school board meeting, a new-member class where interested persons ask about membership requirements in your church, a student council meeting, etc. Make arrangements for your class to sit in on the activity. If possible, ask someone there to brief them on what is happening. Allow plenty of time for this trip and prepare your class beforehand if they need special dress or transportation. Afterwards, plan to review what happened on the trip.

If you have a panel or guest speaker, it's important for the speaker or panel and the class to feel comfortable with one another. Try to create a feeling of ease by your introduction. Ask your class to write down questions they have about law for your special guest. You might collect these while the speaker is talking, or use these questions as the basis for the talk. If no specific talk is prepared, plan to "prime" the speaker with some good starter questions of your own. You might have four or five such questions written down ahead of time. This will give your class a chance to get started thinking. Some ideas to consider might include these:

1. What area of law are you involved with?
2. What is your specific job—do you make laws, change them, enforce them, etc.?
3. Where do the laws you deal with come from? Who made them and when and why?
4. Do you feel the law serves a purpose? What is it?
5. What would happen without these laws?
6. Do you think people need laws? Why?

After the presentation and questioning, summarize in a few sentences what has been said. Thank your guests, and if they are leaving, tell them a little about what the class will be doing the rest of the class period.

The lesson experience

The Ten Commandments are not the main thrust of this chapter. They are included as only one example of law—the kind with broad application rather than a more limited use. There should be other times in your students' course of study when a thorough study of these Commandments will be made. If you are unable to do other outside projects, you might want to use some class time to review the Commandments and Luther's Small Catechism in more detail.

How you construct this lesson will depend on the resources available to you and your interest in doing outside activities. If you have a panel or outside guest, you may want to allow them most of your class period. Remember that the field trip should be conducted outside of class time. At any rate, begin by including any outsiders in your introduction of the week's study and the plan for the lesson.

Whatever decision you make, let your class and any others know from the beginning what you have in mind. If you have a guest speaker or a panel, introduce them to the class with a few words about who they are and why you invited them. Also introduce your class to the guests by explaining who the members of the class are and what they have been studying that prompted this invitation.

This might be a good time for an opening prayer. If you have a class that is now doing well with conversational prayer, suggest that they include your guests and the topic of law, or offer a prayer yourself which asks God to help all of you see the benefit of law in your lives.

List of laws. To give your resource people an idea of where your class is in their thinking about law, ask the students to open their notebooks and report the kinds of laws to which they found they are subject. List these on the board. Some ideas which you might want to help them define more clearly could be:
- civil law—traffic signals, curfews, burglary, shoplifting, etc.
- school law—dress codes, attendance rules, report cards, final exams, credit requirements for graduation, etc.
- home rules—curfew hours, allowances, chores, use of the car or stereo, caring for brothers or sisters, meal responsibilities, etc.
- organization or group rules—they may belong to clubs, the YMCA, Girl Scouts, choir, band, etc. All are run by rules, some formal and some informal.

After you have written their list on the board, spend a few minutes talking about their feelings about laws. It is important to establish where they are and how they see the law. Is it useful? Is it something they resent? What do they think is the purpose of law?

This week's lesson has some things to say about the nature of law and why we need it. Where do they think we would be without laws? Do we have more laws than we need? How do we go about changing laws that are no longer useful to us? These are questions we may not have answers for, but we do want to raise them.

Discuss the chapter. Discuss the three observations about the Old Testament law that should be kept in mind when we look at specific laws. List them on the board and ask your class to include them in their notebooks:

1. The law is a gift from God.
2. God's love came first; the law was a result of that relationship.
3. God created a world that makes sense; the law tells us how to keep it that way.

These are important points to keep in mind when we consider any of the laws that are in the Bible. Most of us are familiar with the Ten Commandments, but we have little knowledge of the many other laws listed there. Some of them we feel we must keep; others we feel don't apply anymore.

Remind your class again that the Bible is both *divine* and *human*. What did we say that means? It is a record of God's relationship with his people, but parts of it may be a word for a certain people at a certain time, not for every people in all times!

Then turn to the biblical examples of the law as listed in your chapter. You could divide the class into three groups to reread these passages, or ask three individual students to read them and report to the class.

1. The Ten Commandments. Here is the best example of laws with eternal significance. They are concerned with broad principles, not specific details. What does the class think about the Ten Commandments? Are they useful? Does the class understand what they mean?
2. The book of the covenant. These laws concern a specific group of people. They were for another time and place.
3. Food laws. These were good laws for those times. Many people feel they no longer need to be followed, although there is disagreement about some of them.

Now that we have examined some of the kinds of laws, how do we deal with them? How does law enter into our relationship with God? How do we know whether or not we are obligated to obey? What guidance has God given us about all laws? This is really a review of the whole lesson.

End the study by reinforcing the fact that God gave us laws to help us maintain order in his creation and for our own good. Many laws change as the world changes, but our relationship with God is not dependent on the keeping of the law—God loves us all the time! The law shows us the kind of conduct that God desires and that helps us to live in harmony with other people.

Closing prayer

Suggest that each student offer a prayer about one particular law that they feel has been good for them (it might be a parent's rule, a traffic light, or a chance to vote in a free country).

Home assignment

This week the students should read all of Chapter 8 and any biblical material included in that chapter in preparation for next week.

The Conquest of Canaan

Objective
The objective of this lesson is to study the events following the escape from Egypt and during the conquest of the promised land.

Biblical basis
Numbers 11–14; Joshua 6:1-21; Judges 2:6—3:30

Background information
A great deal of historical information is covered in this lesson. Look again at your map of the Old Testament world as an aid in reviewing the events in Israelite history leading up to the conquest of Canaan. You may want to reread parts of some of the previous lessons and also the biblical background as a part of your own personal review.

Some difficult questions are raised by this lesson. One concerns the whole idea of God and war. Whose side is God on in any war? There are no easy answers to that question in these stories, but we don't want to avoid the question, either. Give some thought to how you want to explore our ideas about war and whose side God is on and what he leads his people into.

Preparation for class
In order to cover this material in one class period, you may want to divide into smaller groups and ask each group to investigate one section of the lesson material. Two optional activities that you could use to highlight this week's study are 1) a TV box or 2) role playing.

A TV box is a possible way of tying the stories together. You can make one by simply taking a cardboard box and cutting a hole in one side to resemble a TV screen. Make slits along the sides large enough to draw your "film" through. Perhaps you should have the box ready beforehand and let your class spend the time writing and drawing scenes of the saga of the Old Testament conquest.

Another suggestion would be to use role playing as a way of describing the judges God sent to help at appropriate times. Look at these stories again in the reading book and gather a box of appropriate props for role playing them. Also make use of the time line and the Old Testament map to help the class see when and where all of this happened.

The lesson experience
Begin the class by briefly reviewing what was learned about the law in last week's lesson. Emphasize again that the law is a gift from God, meant for our own good.

There was a home assignment of reading the chapter and biblical narrative for this week, but no additional work was requested. Give your class a few minutes to review this reading at the beginning of the hour. The historical overview of the lesson is dependent on their knowledge of what is in the chapter and the Bible stories.

Then give your class a few minutes to review the main themes of this week's chapter. How many of them remember the promises God made to Abraham in our first lessons? Can they name the specific things that God promised he would give Abraham and his descendants *(land, a nation, a blessing)?*

What has happened to those promises so far in our story? This week's story reveals how faithful God is after all this time; once he makes a promise, he never goes back on it! In this lesson we see how God permits his people to occupy the land he promised and also how the nation begins to develop.

Remember the story of the deliverance from Egypt? The people figured they were really "home free" once they got away from Egypt—but that feeling didn't last long. What happened after they got out of Egypt?

Part of what happened to the people is recorded in Numbers 11-14. Here we find them complaining. Because of their complaining and disbelief, the people were forced to wander in the wilderness for 40 (that number again) years, until all those who lacked trust in God had died. Even Moses was not allowed to go into the land that had been promised.

Six important judges. The people counted on God to send a new and effective deliverer whenever things got really bad. And they weren't disappointed. Every time the story looks hopeless, we read about a deliverer that God sent to the people. These deliverers were called *judges*. Remind your class that the Israelites then were a disorganized group of people with no government and without central leadership to keep order and make plans.

Depending on the size of your class, assign one character to each student or group of two or three. They should read the Bible passage about that person and create a brief picture sequence and story of the person's contribution and life. The drawings will be taped together for a TV box and the writing will be read while the TV show goes on. If you would rather do role plays, bring out your box of props and ask each student to work out a brief play sequence describing the action.

1. Ehud—Judg. 3:15-30
2. Deborah—Judges 4-5
3. Gideon—Judges 6-8
4. Jephthah—Judges 11-12
5. Samson—Judges 13-16
6. Samuel—1 Samuel 1-3; 7-11

A few notes about these people are found in the reading book. If the students have difficulty with the Bible story, recheck the chapter. These are exciting stories of heroes, told in down-to-earth language. They have humor and human interest. Encourage the class to use this same kind of style in depicting their character.

Allow time to develop the character studies and then have a class presentation. If you use the TV box, tape the drawings together and show the whole story to the class, letting the students present their own material.

The battle of Jericho. Josh. 6:1-21 is a story which raises some difficult questions. God had decided to give the Israelites the city of Jericho. The battle is a miracle. There is no other way to explain it. Take a minute to talk about what happened at Jericho and what the people had to do to win this battle. Their instructions seemed ridiculous, and yet all they needed to do was to believe God meant for them to win.

Why did God let the people take the city? Does God step in to punish people who are evil? Are there examples of this in the Bible? Can they think of examples from the Bible where evil appears to triumph? Did Jesus fight back? How can we reconcile the idea that evil must be defeated and at the same time that we should overcome evil with good (love)? It is important to use good judgment in deciding when to fight, both on a personal level and as a nation.

It's good to ask hard questions. You can do a lot for your class by allowing them to explore these difficult questions, even though there are no easy answers. There is disagreement among Christians about war and participating in it. No matter what we decide, it is not an easy question, but one that should be raised. How do we decide if our country should take part in a war?

Review. Ask your students to write their answers to these questions in their notebooks. Why were the judges sent to the people? What meaning does this have for us? What difference does it make to us that God sent a deliverer when his people were in desperate trouble, complaining and disobeying? What does it tell us about God?

The writers of Judges are telling the history of their nation. Their point of view is important. Help your students understand that these writers believed good things happened when the people obeyed God and bad things happened when they didn't. We may not agree that it always works out that way, but that is how the writer is telling this story. He sees it in terms of a cycle—the people do wrong, are punished, cry for help, God sends a deliverer, they repent and worship God again, and are blessed.

God's promise of a land is fulfilled in these stories. The second promise is beginning to be fulfilled in the story of Samuel. Review his story, pointing out that he is the last of the judges and the first of the prophets. He's the man who speaks for God in choosing a king. The desire for a king developed over a period of time. Earlier the people felt God was king and there should not be a human king for fear that he—and they—would forget who was really in charge.

What do your students think about the Israelites' desire for a king? Should they have done without one? Was a king necessary if they were to become a nation? This decision marks a new phase in the history of the people of Israel.

Closing prayer

Why not close with conversational prayer, going around the room and having each student offer a sentence prayer? Your prayer can close the session.

Home assignment

Next week we'll talk about the kings who made Israel a nation. Ask your class to prepare by reading Chapter 9 and making a list of qualifications they think a person should have to be king of the people of God.

9
Three Kings and Two Prophets

Objective
The objective of this lesson is to acquaint the student with several Old Testament themes:

1. God cares about the kind of government we have. Rulers are subject to him.
2. The hope for an ideal king begins with David.
3. The kings of Israel were human—they made mistakes and did wrong things, just as we do. But God does not forsake his people, he loves us even when we are disobedient.
4. This is the beginning of the people we call prophets. They are spokesmen for God.

Biblical basis
1 Samuel 9; 16; 17; 2 Samuel 7:1-17; 11:1—12:15; 1 Kings 3:1-28

Background information
Again this lesson covers much material. There could be a lesson built around each of the kings and prophets discussed in this lesson, but we do not have the luxury of that much time. However, encourage students who are sincerely interested to further investigate individual kings and prophets. The course objectives are a good reminder—we are interested in an *overview* of the Bible, seeing it as a story of God and his people, and helping our students to see that they, too, have been chosen by him.

Try not to get frustrated about not covering all the material. Instead, relax and stick to your basic objectives. If certain details and events have to be passed over, trust them to another time or another course. This will free you to go in the direction your students want to take and to explore their questions and interests without a nagging agenda of "too much to cover."

The word *messiah* is mentioned in the chapter. You may want to look it up in a Bible dictionary or other reference book. It stems from the Hebrew, meaning "the anointed one," and the same word in Greek is "Christ." It originally meant anyone anointed, such as a high priest, but gradually came to mean the one anointed by God's representative to be the king. Oil was poured on the head to signify God's choosing that person.

After God promised David that he would always have someone from David's family to be king, and that the kingship would last forever, the word *messiah* came to mean "the representative of the royal line of David." Later, the prophecy began to refer to the ideal king the people needed as a deliverer, empowered by God to lead them. This is the *messianic hope* referred to in our chapter. We believe that Jesus was the fulfillment of that promise to David to send a "king of kings" (note 2 Sam. 7:12-16).

Preparation for class
If you have a cassette tape recorder available, tape interviews with persons who play the roles of Samuel, Saul, David, Solomon, and Nathan. Be sure you have an empty cassette and knowledge of how to operate the recorder. Or you could use the same idea, but instead have a panel of people representing the three kings and two prophets. Further directions for this activity follow.

The lesson experience
Write the words "The ideal king" on the board. This can be an introduction to your discussion about the kings and a reminder of the students' home assignment concerning the qualifications for a king to serve God and his people.

Why not open the class with a prayer, using volunteers from the class? It sometimes is a real help if you plant some ideas about what you'll be doing during the hour as an indication of what they may want to pray about. Start the prayer or end it with a sentence which asks God to lead us in understanding how much he cares about us, even our rulers and leaders, and what a comfort it is to know all leaders are subject to him. Let others contribute as they wish.

Then turn to the notebooks and take a look now at what students have written about qualifications for being king. Place their ideas on the board. Try to get all your students to contribute at least one idea here. Use words or short phrases whenever you can—such as honest, worthy of respect, intelligent, brave.

Ask who some of the kings or leaders are in the world today. How do they measure up against the qualifications on the board? The struggle to find good leaders is not an easy one. From the beginning, the people in the Bible had trouble finding that perfect person they needed to lead them. Some leaders did better than others, but our lesson points out that the people began to hope for a future ideal king.

Now is the time to get into the stories of the three kings and two prophets. Appoint one person to be the interviewer. What questions should be asked of the kings and prophets? Those who play Samuel, Saul, David, Solomon, and Nathan should look into the biblical story and prepare information for the interviewer. Others could use this time to review the chapter and what it says about each of these people. Give the group time to prepare their material, using their reading books and their Bibles.

The material can be presented either as a series of taped interviews or as a panel. You can help the interviewer to ask pointed and important questions about what each person contributed to the life of the Israelites. How do they feel they accomplished what they did? How did they come to be a king or a prophet? How did their relationship with God affect their life? If you wish to involve more people, use a different interviewer for each character.

Add some human interest questions too. What kind of family life did you have? To whom or what do you attribute your great success? What was your lifelong dream? Who were your childhood heroes? What do you consider your weaknesses?

Summarize. After the presentation, review the highlights. What did we learn? Ask your students to use their notebooks while you write short comments on the board to help them. It might look something like the chart on page 39.

As you summarize, remember that these people were only human beings. They were less than perfect. But God loved them, and they became good leaders for him, making important contributions to the welfare of the nation. What can we learn about ourselves from this series of stories? What kind of people does God work through? What does God expect from us? What can we expect from God? Here is an opportunity to personalize the idea that God can use us for his purposes even when we do not always obey.

Another reminder from this lesson is that the writers of these stories also think that the world makes sense. They write from the viewpoint that God is in charge of everything and when things go wrong, it's because people have fallen away from the right relationship with God. They then need reminding of God's promises—so God sends a messenger to tell them what should be done and to warn them about what will happen if people forget him.

Preview of coming divisions. From the chart and the stories in the lesson, we see that things are going downhill with this unified government. Next week's lesson is a description of how Israel lost the opportunity to be a strong and important nation. It's the story of the divided kingdom. Assign your class to read Chapter 10 in the reading book for next week and to write in their notebooks the names of at least two countries or nations they can think of that started out as one unified country and ended up divided. Also they should write a sentence or two about how the division came about (civil war, rebellion against a king, natural boundary changes, etc.).

Old Testament unit quiz—Chapters 6–9. You may want to give the following quiz at the beginning of your next class. It can serve as a summary of Chapters 6–9 and also as an introduction to the new chapter.

1. Name the man who led God's people out of Egypt *(Moses)*.
2. What are two things we learn about God from the story of the Exodus? *(he keeps his promise; he has compassion on the weak and oppressed; he sends a deliverer)*.
3. What is a number we find important in the story of the life of Moses and his work with God's people? *(40)*.
4. How did God want people to view the law he gave them? *(as a gift to help them because he loved them)*.
5. The Ten Commandments are an example of one kind of law we find in the Old Testament—name one other kind found there *(food laws, the book of the covenant)*.
6. What do you think laws are for? *(helping people—keeping order—making sense of the world God created)*.
7. Name two judges God used to help the people of Israel *(Ehud, Deborah, Gideon, Jephthah, Samson, Samuel)*.
8. What did God send the judges to do? *(to help the people obey him; good happened when they did this, and bad things resulted from their sin—the judges were deliverers from this)*.
9. Who was the first king of Israel? *(Saul)*.
10. What do you remember about David from the Bible story of him? *(a warrior, a musician, an adulterer, wrote poetry, repented of his sins)*.

Who / What	SAUL	DAVID	SOLOMON	SAMUEL	NATHAN
How he got to be king (or prophet)	Anointed by Samuel as the first king (1 Sam. 10:1; 11:14)	Anointed by Samuel when God decided to take the throne away from Saul (1 Samuel 16)	David's son and his appointed successor (1 Kings 1:22-40)	His mother promised him to God before he was born (1 Samuel 1–2)	
Personality characteristics	Good soldier; moody	Popular; poet and musician; warrior and hero; religious	Wise; writer	Faithful	Courageous—stood up to David
Important contributions	Won many battles for his people; united people for first time under a king	Unified the nation; captured Jerusalem; beginning of messianic hope	Built temple; showed wisdom (war and trade agreements)		Told the kings of God's word to them to help them in ruling and warned them of the results of disobedience
Problems	Jealousy; moodiness	Had trouble with his sons; guilty of adultery and murder	Forced labor and taxes; allowed idol worship		
Add your own ideas here					

10
The Big Split

Objective
The objective of this lesson is to show how human failures and disobedience brought about a split into two kingdoms. The story of God's people now becomes a story of two nations, not one.

Biblical basis
1 Kings 12:1-15; 17:1-24; 2 Kings 17:1-23

Background information
Carefully read the biblical material covered in this lesson. Reread the chapter in the reading book so you become familiar with the people and events that resulted in the division of the kingdom.

There are not many good times in this lesson. Unfaithfulness to God caused constant wars, quarrels, and finally exile. You may want to skip over all this bad news and concentrate on the miracles of the prophet Elijah, but consider the questions that are raised from the study of such times. This lesson allows students to ask, "What is God doing when his people get in trouble? Doesn't he care about his people? Will God abandon his people when they're unfaithful?"

The miracles of Elijah and his prophecy are found in the midst of the stories of bad times. He is an important figure and one who is worth looking at closely. He is sometimes likened to Jesus, who came in troubled times too.

Preparation for class
It is important for the class to sense the nature of the division that took place in the kingdom of Israel and how drastically it affected the people. One idea for visualizing the two kingdoms might be to hold a contest of some sort. Another idea is to play the game called "Trust," in which two sides seek to outscore each other. In either of these activities, the idea of competing against each other rather than working together is emphasized.

Both activities will be described in the lesson section. Choose whichever you feel most suitable to your needs. Limit these activities to no more than 15 minutes of your class time in order to be able to adequately cover the biblical material. Use your watch. Remind them at 5 minute intervals of the time left and end the game after 15 minutes.

The lesson experience
If you planned a quiz, give it right away, and correct papers in class. Bring some sheets of white paper and several felt-tip markers to class. Begin by asking the students to read what they have in their notebooks about countries they know of that have been divided at one time or another. As they share their information, write in big letters the names of the divided countries on separate pieces of paper. For example, if Germany is mentioned, write East Germany on one piece of paper and West Germany on another.

When everyone has shared, add a few names of your own such as North and South Vietnam, Communist China and Nationalist China, the North and South during the American Civil War, India and Pakistan. When your list is complete, post the first set of papers on one side of the room, the second at the other side of the room. If you have bulletin boards, use that space. Otherwise, simply tape them where everyone can see the two sides. Ask your students about their feelings. Do they sympathize with certain groups listed here? How do they feel about countries that are unable to settle their differences?

Contest. Divide the class into two sides and hold a contest. Ask each side to prepare 20 questions for the other side to answer about people and events studied in the past weeks, using their reading books and their Bibles. They should attempt to use questions which review an idea or event talked about in class. They will receive one point each time a member of the opposite team answers their question correctly! This will give them an incentive to use questions that are not too difficult to answer. However, members of the opposite team will get two points for every correct answer they give! This is a safeguard against questions being too easy.

Give your students time to prepare their questions and answers. Then separate the teams into two groups with yourself stationed between the teams. You will act as the questioner and will keep score for each team. Let the teams alternate in asking questions. When you call time, the team with the most points is the winner.

"Trust." You may decide to skip the contest and play the simple game of "Trust." Isolate your two teams in separate rooms so they can talk freely without the other team overhearing. Use a room close by or next door if possible. Before they divide, give them these simple rules:

The game is called "Trust." The object is to get as many points as you can. All you need is small slips of white paper and a pencil for each team. When your turn comes, your team must decide what they will give to the other team. If you write the word *blue* on your paper, you will give them 5 points to add to their score. If you write the word *red* on the paper, you give them a negative number—minus 10 points—for their score. You have two minutes to take your turn, giving the teacher your paper to deliver to the other team. They then have their turn. There will only be four turns.

Then send your teams to their places to begin playing. Don't repeat the rules. Most people don't listen very carefully and part of the fun and frustration of the game is wondering if they heard right. After the first two turns (one round), post the two team scores where each team can see them. Then begin the second round with the suggestion, "This will be worth a double-point value" (a blue is worth 10 points, a red is a minus 20). The third round should be usual value, then before the fourth round, suggest to each team that they choose a negotiator to talk with one person from the other team and try to make an agreement about points to be awarded in this round. The negotiators will have two minutes to talk, and then decide what color their teams will give. Bring the class together to look at the final score and talk about the game.

What did we learn? The whole point of the contest or the game has to do with what we learn about ourselves. How did your students feel about the side they were on? Did they want their side to win? Did they feel proud? As the game progressed, how did they act? Discuss what you saw happening between members of the same and opposing teams.

Chapter 10 describes a group of people who started out together and ended up divided. They had many problems and we want to take a look at what happened to them in order to see how God dealt with them.

Have the class spend a few minutes reviewing while you write the words *Israel* and *Judah* on the board. Do they know which was the Northern and which the Southern Kingdom? Write these words below the right name. How long did each kingdom exist after the death of Solomon? *(200 years for Israel and about 335 years for Judah).* What happened to them? *(they spent most of their time fighting each other. Finally they were defeated and exiled).*

Into the Bible. Elijah is an important figure. He brought God's promises and warnings to the people of his day and there are a number of similarities be-

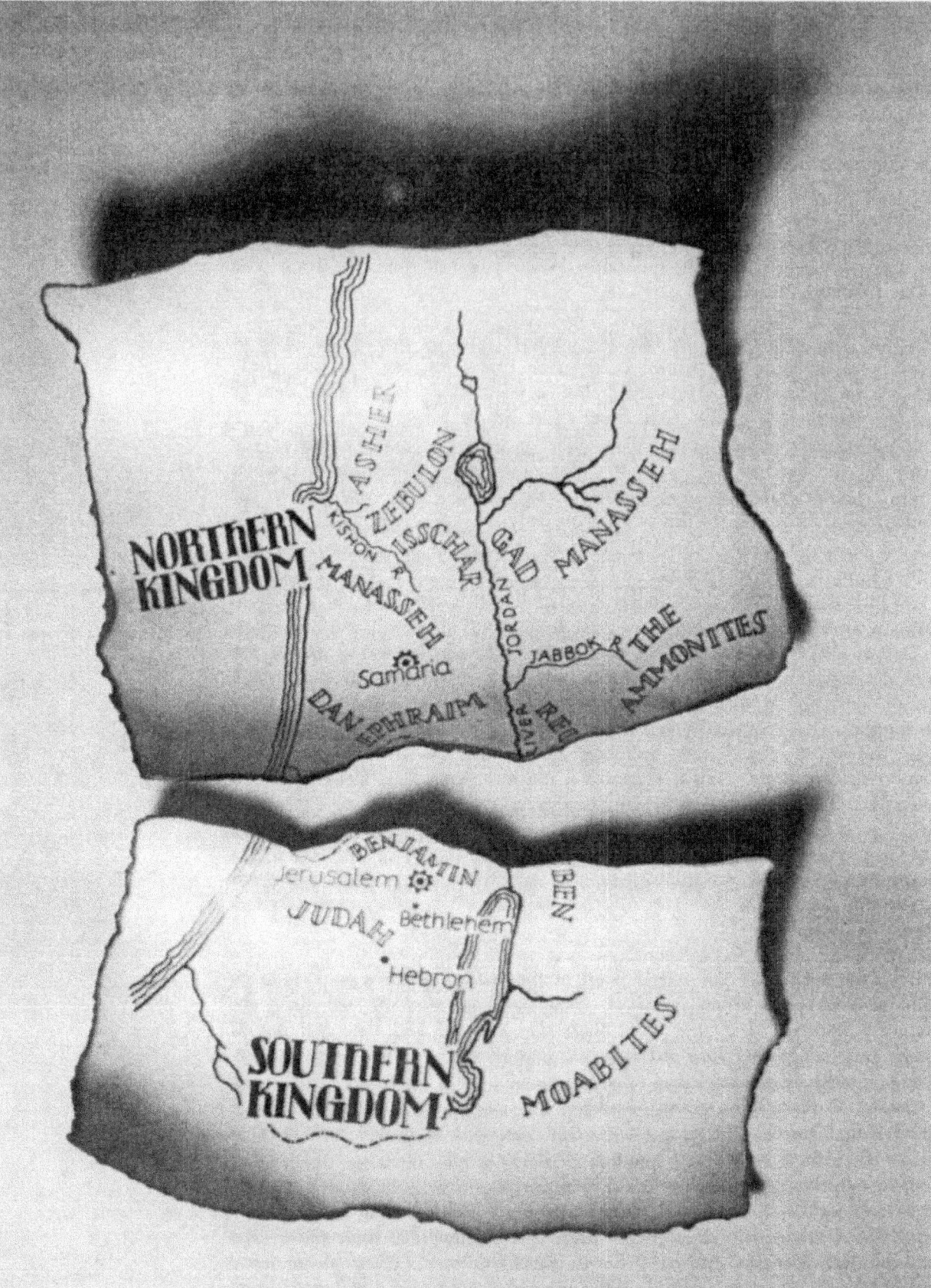

tween his life and that of Jesus. Examine some of the Elijah material. Ask individual students to look up these passages and share what happened:

1 Kings 17:1-7	fed by ravens in wilderness
1 Kings 17:8-16	widow's food multiplies
1 Kings 17:17-24	restores life to dead boy
2 Kings 2:1-18	taken up to heaven
Mal. 4:5-6	return is foretold
Luke 9:28-36	present at transfiguration

This will give you an idea of the special kind of person Elijah was. Talk a little about what Chapter 10 has to say about him. Why is he important to Christians? We'll hear him mentioned again in our New Testament study of Jesus (see Matt. 11:14; 17:11-12).

Call attention to the paragraph about the three places in the Bible where there are many miracles:
1. the time of the exodus
2. the time of Elijah
3. the time of Jesus

How does your class feel about these miracles? What did they think of the reading book suggestion that there are three things we can do about accepting them: we can (1) take them at face value; (2) try to give a logical explanation; or (3) admit there's something of a mystery in them and concentrate on understanding what the story tells us about God.

Then turn to 2 Kings 17:1-23 and have class members read it aloud. Here we have the details of what happened to the Northern Kingdom of Israel. The writers of the biblical story want to give a reason as to why this happened. After reading this aloud, review the six points that are made in the student book at the end of Chapter 10.

The kingdom and the land are gone. The logical question is "What happens now?" How is God going to keep all those promises he had made? How does the class react to this chapter? Why do they think the kingdom ended up as it did? What can we learn from this kind of story?

Closing prayer

Close this lesson with silent prayer. You might give some prayer suggestions about the ideas covered this week and the things we might have learned about ourselves.

Home assignment

Ask the students to read Chapter 11 of their reading book before coming to class next week. In their notebooks, ask them to write a description and draw a picture of a prophet. All students should come to class with the name of at least one person from life today whom they consider to be a prophet. As the teacher, you should do this also.

Gloomy Prophets

Objective
The objective of this lesson is to look at some Old Testament prophets and their messages and to see what we can learn about these prophets for our own lives.

Biblical basis
Amos 5:14-15; 8; Ezekiel 2:1-5; Hosea 11

Background information
In teaching this lesson it will be important for you to read and reread the chapter and the biblical material covered in the chapter. It is good to remember that God provides for us in what he knows is best for us at the time. If he has something to say to his people, he asks someone to give them that message. At times that is a comforting and hopeful bit of news, but at other times it might be a message that causes us to squirm about some of the things that we do, and it may call us to change the way we live.

The prophets had a difficult task. They were asked to deliver stern messages. Often their messages were not very popular. Why should they be believed? How can we tell a real prophet from a phony one? To whom should we listen to learn what God wants us to do? The truth is that only time will tell whether someone is speaking the truth. We can, however, ask if the prophet is telling us to do something contrary to what God has already said is right. Or is he calling us to look again at the plan God formerly laid out, and saying that we ourselves have deserted or altered it to fit our own ideas?

Preparation for class
Be sure to bring some large sheets of art paper to class with which students can illustrate what they think a prophet is, and also for making the repentance charts.

The lesson experience
Open with prayer. By now you have probably worked out a pattern, and your class will know what to expect. If you assign a student to prayer responsibilities each week, call on that person. If all students contribute, suggest that they consider the lessons we have completed thus far and what we have learned about being God's people. You could end the prayer, adding thanks for the special gift of messengers to help us know what it is God wants us to do.

Checking the notebooks periodically is a good way for you to see whether each student is picking up the main concepts and words with which each lesson is dealing. You can do this as they come to class. You are not interested in correcting the notebooks but in finding out if your students are getting the main points and writing down words, ideas, and images that are central to the lesson objectives. You will notice that each book is different—encourage this.

Try to learn something about your students by glancing at each book. It will tell you who is bored, attentive, slower, etc. If a notebook is almost completely blank, an individual conference might be arranged to see what the problem is.

Begin the actual lesson by asking the students to open their reading books to Chapter 11 and briefly review what they have read about the prophets. Give only a minute or two for this—they should have read this material at home and you will cover some of it again in class experiences.

What did they think of the story of the stranger in church on Christmas morning? How would they have felt if they had been present? Would they have been surprised—or irritated with his insistence that they change their life-style? Do they know anyone like the person in the story? Have they heard or read stories about such strange prophets before? If so, encourage your students to tell about it. This is the place to turn to last week's assignment concerning their descriptions and drawings of a prophet.

Some of the Old Testament prophets were similar to this stranger in church. They made pests of themselves, coming around with bad news for God's people. Sometimes, of course, the news was good, but more often at this period of history it was a word to make people uncomfortable and willing to change.

Remind the class that we met our first prophets in the stories about the beginning of kingship. Remember Samuel, Nathan, and Elijah? They advised the kings and people and were the first of this group of messengers God used to bring his word to his people.

Ask your students to include the names of other prophets in their notebooks. Then share them aloud and write them on the board so everyone becomes familiar with their names. Some of them were Isaiah, Jeremiah, Ezekiel, Hosea, and Amos. All of these have their words recorded in the Bible in books that are named after them. Take a minute to find these five books in the Bible.

But how can you tell a real prophet? Our chapter points out that it isn't easy. Sometimes only time will tell who was speaking for God. Evidently each prophet had a direct experience with God that convinced him he must speak out. Can your students recall some of these experiences? If not, open your Bibles to these passages and read them as a class.

Why did God send prophets with a message of doom? Read Amos 5:14-15 and Ezek. 2:1-5. Talk a little bit about the fact that God warns us when we are headed in the wrong direction. There is always a chance that we will listen to what he says and change our ways—he wants us to repent.

Repent is a word for the notebooks. Do your students know its meaning? Write it on the board. Can they think of synonyms for it? What causes people to repent? Perhaps you can look it up in a Bible dictionary. Try to get the concepts of *regret* and *change* into your working definition. These are the things the prophets were looking for from God's chosen people.

Ask your students if they have ever done something they really regretted. If so, why did they regret it? What did they do about it? Would they say they had *repented*? Change is essential for repentance. The prophets warned the people they must change or it would indicate their repentance was not real. Change was a sign of hope. When the prophets didn't see people changing, they knew the message hadn't been taken to heart.

How about us? What does this lesson mean for us? We need to apply the prophets' message to our own lives. There are several activities that will help us to see ourselves and understand how God speaks to us and how we listen.

First, hand out sheets of art paper. Describe this activity as a chance to picture in our mind's eye what a prophet actually is. Ask the students to close their eyes and think about these things:
- How does somebody get to be a prophet?
- Why would God need or use a prophet anyway?
- What is the work he is called to do?
- What words describe his message?
- What pictures come to mind concerning a prophet and his message?
- What happens if people listen to a prophet?

After they have thought about these for a minute, ask them to picture on paper the kinds of things they associate with a prophet. They shouldn't worry about being artists. Encourage them to use their own ideas to interpret what they have just read. Give them 5 to 10 minutes. Pictures should be simple. They can include words as well as images. They don't have to include people. Then let students share what they have done, asking each one to describe briefly the symbols and what they mean.

Repentance cycle

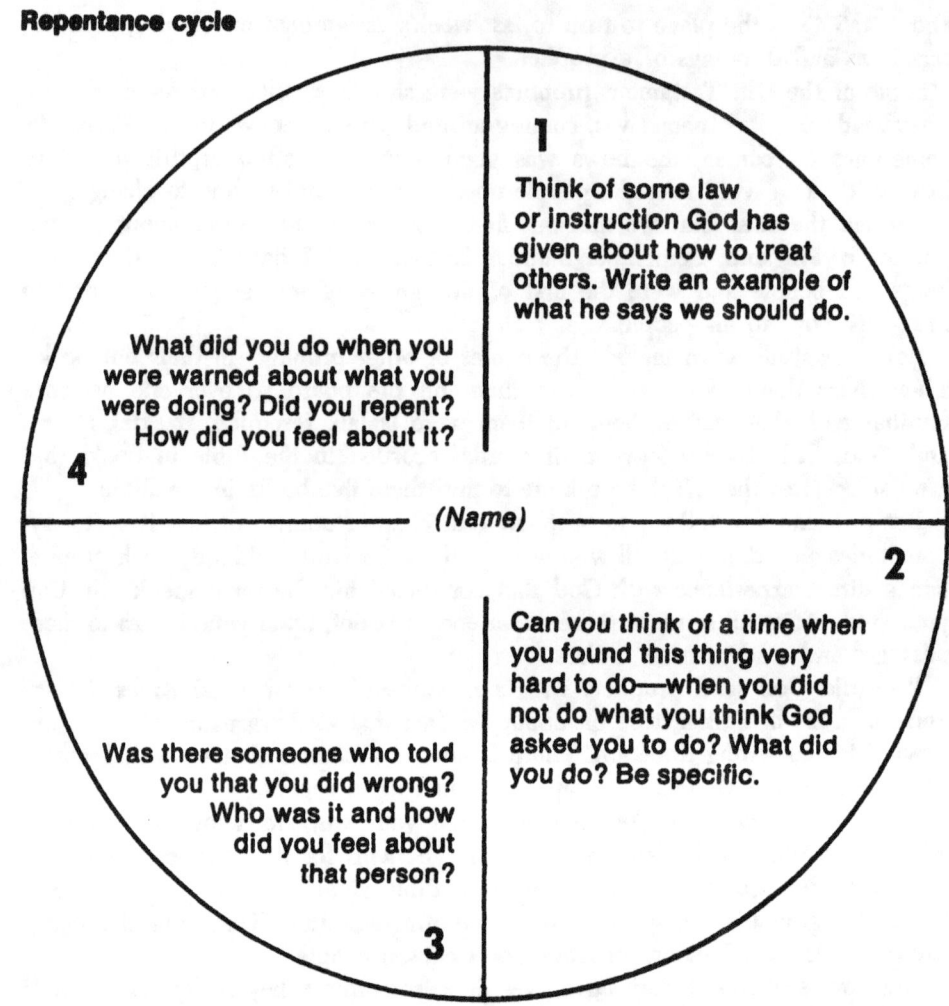

If there is time, do the *repentance cycle*. Since one of the central themes of the prophets has to do with change, this activity is designed to give the student an opportunity to reflect on the word and its meaning for us. Explain that each of us is to think about something we did wrong and someone who served as a sort of prophet to us, bringing us to repent.

Give each student a blank sheet of paper. In the middle, ask that they draw a circle and print their first name in it. Then they should draw lines to divide the circle into four quarters. Each section should contain their answers to the questions. The answers should be personal and should deal with something that really happened. The event in Section 2 should be as recent as possible. You can reproduce this cycle on the board and write the questions in so everyone can see them. They should begin with Section 1.

The cycle of repentance is something they may want to think about during the next week. They may reflect on certain people who have helped them to see God's way by pointing out wrong and helping them to change. The people of the Old Testament had the opportunity to listen to the prophets and change. We shall see in the next lesson that they decided to continue in their own ways. This resulted in great suffering and confusion.

Home assignment

Ask the students to read Chapter 12 for next week, listing any signs of hope they find in the chapter or in the Bible readings. Also have them list signs of hope that they see for our world today.

Objective

The objective of this lesson is to study the period of the exile of God's people, by reading some of the ancient biblical passages that speak about it. It was a difficult time and caused God's people to ask some hard questions, particularly concerning what he had in mind for his "chosen" people.

Biblical basis

Isaiah 45:18-25; Habakkuk 1:12—2:4; 2 Kings 25:27-30; Ezekiel 10:18-19; 11:22-25; Jeremiah 14:19-22; Lamentations 5

Background information

This lesson centers on some questions that many of us have wondered about, but may not have expressed aloud. Questions like: Where is God when I feel disappointed, deserted, and lonely? Does God care about me when I have more trouble than I seem to deserve? How do I know? How can I "hang in there" when the going gets rough? Does God punish people?

There are no easy answers. Try to create the atmosphere that it's all right to ask these difficult questions. And don't feel that you need to be the person with the answers. You can say "I don't know" or "There is no easy answer to that one" and be absolutely right. That doesn't mean you don't have faith, or aren't a good teacher—quite the contrary. It may show you have a faith that dares to ask hard questions and are a teacher who continues to learn.

The exile is that time following the end of the two kingdoms: after the Northern Kingdom (Israel) was destroyed in 722 B.C. and the Southern Kingdom (Judah) fell to the Babylonians in 587 B.C. Everything that represented God's people seemingly disappeared. Even the divided nation was gone. The people and the king were sent away. Jerusalem was in ruins, the temple destroyed. It really looked as though God had given up hope—for good.

You might find it helpful to do some outside reading on the exile. At least consult a Bible dictionary. Any information you find about the Babylonians would be helpful, too.

Preparation for class

Try having your class meet in a completely different area of the church from your usual classroom. Arrange to have another teacher or parent in your classroom or in the hall to help your students find their way to their new setting. Post a sign on your board or on the door which says "This Class Moved to (wherever your new meeting place is). All Students Report There Immediately." This notice should be as curt as possible, leaving the impression that someone has *ordered* the class moved from one place to another and right away.

Plan an *exile trip* around the church. You be the leader so you know where you are going and so that no one will be misled or injured. Walk through the areas in advance. Bring handkerchiefs or rags to blindfold each student.

The lesson experience

As your students arrive, they will find their familiar setting for class deserted. Only a written order or an unfamiliar person will be there, giving them instructions on where the class will meet. The idea is to create some of the anxiety that confronts people when they leave familiar surroundings for a strange place.

Once the students have found you in the new setting, don't let them get comfortable. Have them put down their materials and blindfold them for the trip you want to take them on.

The only instructions you need to give are that you plan to take them on a trip and that each student should be blindfolded so that he learns to trust his other senses. He will be dependent upon his leader. Ask that they line up single

Hope in the Midst of Disaster

file and hold hands throughout the trip. Tell them to be aware of how they feel about the whole thing. After everyone is blindfolded and holding hands, take the hand of the first in line and begin the trip. There should be no talking except to give instructions.

Take your line of students to as many different types of rooms and settings as you can: furnace room, balcony, office, narthex. Lead them slowly at times, then quicken the pace, watching to make sure nobody falls. Force them to move faster behind you. If someone drops a hand, stop until the line is complete again. Do little or no talking except to give necessary instructions. Take them up stairs and down stairs; sit down, stand up; go through narrow places, large rooms, etc. Stop at a fountain and offer each a drink. See if you can expose them to some noises, perhaps another class talking or laughing, as well as a quiet place, maybe in the sanctuary. Then return to your usual classroom and unmask them.

Before you discuss the trip, ask each student to write a poem in his or her notebook about the experience, including the fact that the usual room was empty. The poem need not rhyme. It can be as short or as long as necessary to describe what the person felt about himself, others, the space and places involved, etc. While they are writing their poetry, write the word *exile* in large print on the board.

Spend no more than 10 minutes in writing the poetry. Then ask several of the students to read their poems aloud to the class. When everyone who wishes has shared, direct the group into asking and discussing some of these questions:

1. What is it like to be moved from a familiar place to an unfamiliar one?
2. How does it feel to be dependent on someone else to take you someplace?
3. What do you think about when you don't know where you are or where you're going?
4. What do you count on when you are without the usual things you use to get you somewhere? *(sight, instructions, words, etc.)*.
5. How did you feel when you recognized something along the way?

You may have other questions of your own to use. Allow time for students to vent their reactions to this experience and to probe a little deeper into the frustration, anger, discovery, and fright that they felt.

Perhaps they can think of other experiences they have had that were similar to this. Have they played games like this before? Have they ever been lost? Were any of them away from home and homesick? Did any group ever leave them behind by mistake? All of us have had something like this happen to us.

This is your chance to make the exile real. "Many of the things we felt today are the things God's people felt in the lesson for this week—the exile was a time of disappointment, fear, grumbling, stumbling, confusion, and questions about where God's people were going and where God was taking them."

Alternate activity. If the exile trip is not feasible for you, you might use a research project in which the students read articles in newspapers and magazines about people who are exiled. It would be helpful if you could supply some resource material about an exiled group of people. Gather news items from newspapers or magazines, or find research or reference materials under *exiles* in the library. Bring what you can find to class and give the students some time to read about these people.

Then raise questions. Can they share what these people had to say about the experience of being exiled? How did they feel about the people or the cause for their exile? Were they anxious to come home? How did they survive? Do the students know of other people who have been exiled?

Turn to the reading books. Give your class a few minutes to review the material in Chapter 12 and then discuss some of the questions asked. Put yourself in the place of the exiled people as you think about the questions.

1. Is God really the all-powerful creator we thought he was before the exile happened? Read aloud Isa. 45:18-25. The author is attempting to answer this question. What do the students think the answer is?

2. Can God be trusted after all of this disaster? Has he finally given up on us and decided not to keep his promises? Read aloud Hab. 1:12—2:4. What kinds of answers did Habakkuk get from God when he was asking this question?

3. Can we survive without a king—a place to worship—a country? Read aloud 2 Kings 25:27-30; Ezek. 10:18-19 and 11:22-25. What good news about the king and about God is found in these passages?

4. When will all this end? Some of the Bible passages are laments—cries of people who feel the punishment should end and who are beginning to wonder if God will ever send relief. Read aloud Jer. 14:19-22 and Lamentations 5.

5. The Bible says to us that God is at hand, working for us and with us, even in the hard times. We need to hear this message, especially when we're asking these kinds of questions. Discuss signs of hope in our world today.

Closing prayer

Maybe this would be a good week to use a "popcorn" prayer, in which anyone who wants to add something "pops" in whenever they feel like it. Since you began depending on each other in this way, why not end in a circle of clasped hands. Begin the prayer by saying, "Thanks, God, for being with us when we are unsure. . . ." End it when everyone has had a chance to contribute.

Home assignment

Ask the students to prepare for the next class by reading Chapter 13 in the reading book and the biblical material included in that chapter.

They should also interview three people, using this open-ended sentence, "What the world needs now is . . ."

13
Living in Hope

Objective
The objective of this lesson is to emphasize hope. In the midst of despair, God sends messengers of hope. Because he knows what is best for us, we, too, can dare to be hopeful.

Biblical basis
Isaiah 9:6-7; 11:1-5; 53; 61:1-4; Zechariah 9:9-10; Ezekiel 43:1-12; Jeremiah 31:31-34; Daniel 12:1-13

Background information
In this lesson we look at the message of some of the prophets to better understand what they hoped God would do for the world. These prophets had a variety of ideas as to what God might do, but all of them brought words of hope to people who very much needed them.

The word *messiah* is important because it is central to the hope of God's people. Remember that this was the word which came to mean "the ideal king," the "anointed one of God" who would restore the days of David and make them better than ever. Isa. 61:1 speaks of the anointed one as a prophet rather than as a king. Many years later when Jesus read this passage in the synagogue (Luke 4:16-21), he told the people it was being fulfilled in their very midst.

We all have our ideas of what it would take to make a perfect world. Your students will have theirs too. Little wonder that many people found Jesus different from the *messiah* they were expecting! Remember this lesson when we get into the New Testament material and meet the opposition to Jesus from people who had other ideas as to what the Messiah would be like.

Preparation for class
Collect some junk items that can be used in making things—empty pie plates, detergent bottles, toilet paper rolls, Popsicle sticks, small boxes, thread spools, fabric pieces, string, yarn, toothpicks, old magazines and newspapers, magic markers, crayons, scissors, glue, felt scraps, etc. Save these in a box to bring them to class when you need them, or leave them in your room for easy access. They may be used many times for creative projects.

Obtain a cassette recorder with a blank tape. Interview a number of people who are quite different from each other as to age, occupation, and interests. Ask them simply to think for a second and then respond to the question, "What the world needs now is . . ." Your students have been assigned to ask three people this same question, so try to ask people other than those they will be seeking out. Save the tape as a starter for your class. Try to locate a copy of the music to the song "What the world needs now is love, sweet love," either in sheet music or on a recording. It could be used simply to point out one person's view of hope for the world.

The lesson experience
If you have found a recording of the song to use, you might have it playing as the students arrive. Ask your students to share the interviews they recorded in their notebooks about "What the world needs now is . . ." After they have had an opportunity to share the responses they got, play your tape and tell them a little about the people you interviewed. You might want to list on the board some of the key words or phrases they heard people using. Suggest they get their notebooks out and jot down a few of the ideas others found in their interviews.

Introducing the chapter. Begin the chapter by reminding the class that the story of God's people is recorded for us in order to communicate what the writers knew about God and how he was working among them. When times were difficult and people were afraid, God sent messengers called prophets to bring a message of hope and comfort, and a promise that life would get better.

Give the class a few minutes to look at the chapter again. While they are doing this, write the numbers one to six on the board. These numbers will be for listing the students' summaries of the six kinds of hope expressed by the Old Testament prophets and dealt with in our chapter. Leave on the board what they have already listed from their interviews.

Assign each of the hopes found in the lesson to a student or two students together. Let them use the chapter and their Bible. After reading the paragraph and the biblical passages connected with it, ask each group to write a phrase or sentence which summarizes the hope, just as was done for the hopes expressed by the people that were interviewed.

When they have finished, go around the class and call on each one to describe what the chapter said, to read one passage which points out that prophet's idea, and to write their summary phrase or sentence on the board. Suggest that they think up their own rather than simply copy the words they may have found in the chapter. Your list will be a restatement of the six kinds of hope found in the chapter. Some of these topics are very practical suggestions for change, while others are idealistic and not so easy to summarize.

Do the students have some thoughts about which kind of hope would be the best solution for the world? Do they have other ideas of their own that are not listed on either side of the board?

Compare the list that resulted from your discussion of the interviews with the list you got from the chapter and Bible research. Are there any similarities? Differences? Is there one right answer for what God should do to make things perfect again? When Jesus came, did the Jews feel he was the fulfillment of their hopes?

Look at the list again—for many, Jesus was a disappointment. They were looking for something quite different. Do we still need hope? Now that Jesus has been here, is everything perfect again? What need do we have for hope? What does the world still need?

We may not be able to agree on just what God should do or just what the world needs most, but one thing is certain—we could use help! It's apparent that most people feel things could be improved.

Symbol of hope. If there is time, provide a box of materials and ask the class to create a "symbol of hope." They can use ideas from the lists made by the class, or their own feelings about how God will fulfill his promises to his people. It can be a collage, or something they build from scraps and items in the box. Give them adequate time to develop their own ideas for a symbol of hope. Help them by encouraging them to verbalize their thoughts as they work and praising them for beginning attempts at making concrete some of the concepts we've talked about.

Remember in creative efforts like this that some students will feel they can't do anything creative or original. They should be encouraged to try; help them in any way you can. Acceptance of their first efforts is important. Work at having a relationship of acceptance with your class. Each person counts. His or her ideas are valid and deserve expression and acceptance as much as those of the next person. Although some of us are better at such projects than others, everyone is capable of expressing ideas in a creative way if allowed freedom and encouragement. Projects are to be shared, not evaluated or criticized. They should be seen as an extension of ourselves and our ideas and, as such, valuable.

Share the projects after they are finished. Ask each student to give a quick summary of the concept of hope portrayed by the symbol and to explain why this particular concept was chosen.

Consider displaying these creative efforts where members of the congregation can see them and enjoy what is happening in your class. Perhaps your pastor could suggest a place that would allow many to view them, or he might even consider using them as a sermon illustration.

Prayers of hope. As a closing activity, ask each student to write a short prayer that speaks of hope, using ideas talked about in the class. It should be personal—perhaps what they hope for in this world and a request that God would help us trust his promises to us. Or, if time is short, make this a part of your home assignment. If the prayers are completed in class, they could be used as a closing prayer.

Home assignment

Ask the students to read Chapter 14 and the biblical material included in that chapter in preparation for next week's class. Using their notebooks, ask them to write a short paragraph describing a homecoming or a return to some place where they once lived.

You could also assign a short test over Chapters 10–13 to be given at the beginning of the next class period.

The Survivors Return

Objective

The objective of this lesson is to highlight what happened to the people of God when they returned from exile and rebuilt the city and temple at Jerusalem.

1. On the one hand, we see a number of important accomplishments and a fulfillment of promises God had made.

2. On the other hand, we see that not all expectations were completed. There were promises which were not fulfilled, and certain problems arose too.

Biblical basis

Ezra 1:1-5; 10:1-5; Haggai 1:1-11; Zechariah 1:7-17; Nehemiah 8:1-8

Background information

This is an important lesson because of the historical material it covers, and also because it points up a number of issues which remain important to Jews and Christians today.

You may want to choose certain issues raised in this lesson to use as part of your class work. This will depend on your own interests and background and how much time you have for your class. Try to include a thorough review of material in the chapter in terms of accomplishments and problems presented.

The return to the land is an example of a concept on which you could spend some time. It was extremely important to the Jews to have their land. Israel was the land God had promised them. Something similar occurred again in modern times when the new state of Israel was created in 1949. You could gather some materials about this modern-day restoration and investigate the issues involved. War, conflict, hard work, and sacrifice have been part of the Jews' struggle for the land. The lengthy struggle between Jews and Arabs continues.

The rebuilding of the temple is an event you might want to investigate further. How did the temple look when it was originally built by Solomon? What was different about the reconstructed temple? By the time of Jesus, Herod had rebuilt the temple on the same site. Many important New Testament events happened around it. For the Jews the temple was the dwelling place of God, the visible center of their religion.

This is the time also when we first hear about a collection of writings called the law of Moses. During the exile Jewish scholars began collecting materials that were a record of what had happened between God and his people, so that the stories, poems, and prophecies would not be lost. You might bring Bible dictionaries and commentaries to class and try to piece together some information about what eventually became the Old Testament. This could be an interesting area to explore.

Preparation for class

How you prepare for class will depend on which particular issues of this lesson you are interested in emphasizing. If you want to do a research and discovery project on the land, you'll need to gather history and news items about Israel and its various stages of development. There are a number of films and filmstrips which could be used with this study. Or if you know someone who has visited Israel recently, he or she could be used as a resource.

To pursue the idea of the rebuilding of the temple, consider drawing or building a replica of the temple itself. Use whatever materials you have, research the actual measurements, see if you can obtain a sketch or pictures of the temple. Maybe someone in your community has already built a scale model of it. Another possibility is visiting a synagogue in your community and comparing it to the Old Testament temple.

The concept of the Bible's beginnings during this time could be made a focal point of this lesson. Showing a filmstrip outlining the development of the Bible up to the present time might be helpful. You could gather a number of different Bibles and compare them. You could bring published items about the history of such things as the Dead Sea Scrolls, the Septuagint (the Greek Old Testament), the Vulgate (a Latin Bible), etc. Exploring these items together, your class could begin to see the importance of preserving the biblical writings. They could develop a greater appreciation for the Scriptures and their place in the history of God's people.

The lesson experience

Begin with prayer. Remember those prayers of hope that were the last activity of the last lesson? Perhaps you didn't have time to complete them, or you may have assigned them to be written in the notebooks for this week. They could serve as a good way to begin this class.

Review what has happened in the story of God's people. Take a few minutes to make sure every student has an up-to-date picture of your progress through the Old Testament. You can turn to the time line and begin with the time of the divided kingdom. Let them scan their reading books to refresh their memories, or prompt them with certain names, events, and words. At this point, you may want to give the following quiz on Chapters 10–13 and quickly check it in class when they have finished.

1. What were the names of the two kingdoms? *(Israel and Judah)*.

2. Name the great prophet who brought God's promises during this time *(Elijah)*.

3. Name one of the three times and places in the Bible where there are many miracles *(the time of the exodus, the time of Elijah, the time of Jesus)*.

4. Name two prophets who brought bad news to the people about times to come and good news that God still loved them *(Isaiah, Elijah, Jeremiah, Ezekiel, Hosea, Amos, etc.)*.

5. What does "repent" mean? *(to turn around and change one's actions)*.

6. What word describes the time God's people spent as captives living in a foreign land? *(exile)*.

7. What words would you use to describe how God's people felt in a foreign land? *(fear, sadness, disappointment, grumbling, mistrust, etc.)*.

8. What two kinds of leaders did the people hope for during these times? *(one who was a strong soldier, one who could feed them, one who was loving, etc.)*.

9. Why was the destruction of their temple so hurtful to God's people? *(The temple was a visible sign of God's presence with them and his promises to them.)*

10. Who do you think is the hope of our world? *(Jesus)*.

Looking at the chapter. Part of this week's assignment was for students to recall an occasion when they returned to a place after moving away and how they felt about such a homecoming. Can your students share some experiences about moving away? Did they ever return for a visit to a former home? What were their feelings about the return—had things really changed? Often we find that things are not as we remember them. Things change, and so do we! Our lesson this week reminds us that we shouldn't expect time to stand still, or people to stay the same.

Give the class a few minutes to scan the chapter assigned for this week. While they are doing this, divide your chalkboard into two parts with a vertical line. On the left side, in large print, write *Progress*. On the right side, *Problems*.

Be sure to mention the Persian king Cyrus who made it possible for the prophets' words about the return home to come true. Read Ezra 1:1-5 aloud. This is the order of Cyrus that Jews who wished to return to Jerusalem and rebuild their temple could do so.

The Bible books that speak about this time in history are Ezra, Nehemiah, Haggai, and Zechariah. Point out that these weren't always happy times. Many people were deeply disappointed because things had changed. It was a time for beginning again, and new starts can be difficult.

Our chapter talks about three specific areas of accomplishment that we want to look at. Can your students list them? Write them on the board and have your students write them in their notebooks: (1) the return home, (2) the temple rebuilt, and (3) the Bible begun. As you write each of these on the board, briefly discuss what happened and why it is important:

1. The return home was no small accomplishment. For the Jew, nothing could take the place of his homeland. As Christians, we find Israel important in our heritage, too. This was the land where Jesus lived and where many of the biblical events happened.

2. The temple was the center of worship and so its rebuilding was important. Rebuilding, however, was hard work. Haggai and Zechariah spoke important words of encouragement which rallied the people. Nehemiah helped them build a protective wall to make survival possible.

3. In these stories we first hear about a collection of writings, some very old, that are actually the beginnings of the Bible. Ezra brought them with him from Babylon. They served as a link between the past and hopes for the future.

These were some of the good things that happened. But, as always, there were problems too. Write these on the board and in the notebooks and talk about them as you do: (1) isolationism, (2) legalism, and (3) disappointment.

1. These people were concerned with not losing their identity. This was a natural reaction to the situation in exile. Ezra 10:1-5 is an example of what the people were willing to do to keep their people "pure."

The biblical books of Jonah and Ruth may have been written at this time. They both speak against narrowness and emphasize that God is the God of all the world and that his people have a mission to be a blessing to all humanity.

2. Concerning legalism, people were careful to do exactly what the law said, giving little room for personal freedom and decisions. They didn't want something as awful as the exile to happen again.

People can get into deep trouble when they see the law as something we do in order to gain God's favor. Remember that it was given as a guide by God after he had declared and showed his love for people.

3. Some of the returning Jews were disappointed in their restored land. They wanted complete fulfillment of all God's promises. The return was only a partial fulfillment. God would certainly do more—wouldn't he?

Once you have had a chance to cover these points with your class, you can use the time remaining for an in-depth look at one of the areas we talked about earlier. Choose one creative project to highlight one of the accomplishments, or spend some time with the books of Jonah and Ruth, contrasting their stories with the problem of isolationism.

If you wish to probe into more than one of these ideas, divide the class into smaller groups and assign each group one specific area. Spend the remainder of your class time developing these ideas and talking about their significance in the story of God's people up to the present time.

If there is no class time for these projects now, they are topics which are always interesting as individual assignments. Ask if a student or two would volunteer to do research and report to the next class.

Home assignment

Ask the students to read Chapter 15 in their reading book and any biblical material included in it before they come to class next week.

Stories, Songs, and Wisdom

Objective

The objective of this lesson is to introduce the student to other kinds of writing in the Bible:

1. story
2. song
3. wisdom

These writings are examples of human response. That is, rather than emphasizing what God is doing with and for his people, these writings focus on sharing our hopes, dreams, thoughts, and feelings with God.

Biblical basis

Psalm 22; 150; Song of Solomon 2:8-17; Proverbs 15; Ecclesiastes 1:1-11; 3:1-9

Background information

This can be an exciting lesson! It's a chance to take a breather from the narrative history line we've been following, and be introduced to some other kinds of Old Testament biblical literature.

Much of the material you will be dealing with in this week's chapter is unfamiliar to your students, with the possible exception of the book of Psalms. So there is the opportunity of discovery in this lesson.

Another advantage of this lesson is its focus on our response to God. Much of our story so far has dealt with God and his work with his people. This lesson deals with the whole spectrum of the feelings and experiences we have as humans.

Here's another important idea: It's good to be honest with God. This lesson points out clearly that we can't fool God about our attitude toward him and we shouldn't try. When we have problems, complaints, or questions, it's appropriate to come right out and tell him so. This does away with the idea that only certain language and subjects are appropriate for prayer or Christian conversation, and emphasizes the idea of bringing everything to God and doing it with honesty.

Preparation for class

This could be a class session in which you spend time on creative writing, attempting to put down hopes, thoughts, and feelings about God and his work in our life. You could combine the chapter's contents with this creative effort and then share what has been done.

Gather materials for writing—paper, pencils, felt-tip markers, and poster board (for writing songs in large print). And get hold of a record player and any records that would be good background music for poetry or storytelling, a cassette recorder if you have one available, colored construction paper, and anything else that would add some dimensions to expressing our feelings.

The lesson experience

As the students arrive, divide them into three groups, to correspond with the three categories in the chapter. Explain that we want to concentrate this week on the experience of writing in response to what God has done for us—just as those early writers did in the Bible. Then give some guidelines for beginning.

Stories. One part of the class will work on *stories.* They can work as a group or individually as storytellers. Their assignment is to reread that section of the chapter in the reading book, and to read the books of Jonah or Ruth in the Bible. This will give them an idea for writing a story which explains some important truth about who God is or what it is like to be a human being.

The story they write should tell about some person and this person's response to God and the world around him or her. It should convey an important truth they have learned about God, and include some insights into how people feel about their experiences, and how they might express themselves to God.

Songs. Another third of the class members should work on *songs*. They can reread the section on songs in the chapter, and the biblical material included in it. Then they are to write a song. It could be a lament, bringing their pains and anxieties to God and others, or a song of joy about something that's happening—whatever is real for them. It should be honest, an expression of where life and God are for them. It could be a love song like the Song of Solomon, a song of praise, one of anticipation for the coming of God's Messiah, or whatever they want it to be.

Wisdom. This will be the topic for the last third of the class. They can reread the section of the chapter with that title and the biblical material suggested within it. Their task is to write wisdom. They are to raise questions and seek answers using the commonsense kind of sayings found in Proverbs. They will have to try to express some sort of "life stance" as they have observed it—to make some sense of what is going on around them and be honest with God concerning how they feel. Their reflections shouldn't be idealistic laws about what we should or shouldn't do, but an honest suggestion of how things are and why. They can read a number of chapters in Proverbs to get further into the idea, if they have trouble getting started.

All groups should be encouraged to write down words, thoughts, and phrases as they come to mind. No set pattern is required for their project. They can use whatever materials they choose, or music, or tape. They will be sharing what they write and should know this from the beginning. Also it might be helpful to picture themselves as a group of Old Testament writers trying to respond to God in their own individual ways, but also trying to communicate their experiences to others.

Allow time for enjoying the project and working seriously on creating something that will be an honest expression of the way they see God in their life right now.

Give the groups a chance to share their work, or if everyone worked separately, ask volunteers to read their own material. Some may have a song. Did they put it to music? (Someone might think of starting with a familiar tune like "Jingle Bells" and writing lyrics to go with it.) What's the song about? Can they teach it to the class? The sharing time should be accepting, but also relaxed and fun. There will be room for humor and good-natured jest if the setting is informal and you give the impression that we can all enjoy ourselves.

This sharing time is also review time. Ask your students to make a few notes in their notebooks about what they learned about each category through their work or the sharing of others.

Review the chapter. After everyone has had a chance to share, review the chapter, picking up any important items about this part of the Bible that may have been missed. Ask a few questions to make sure the students understood these kinds of writings.

1. How are the stories we read about in this chapter different from the stories of Abraham, Isaac, Jacob, and Joseph? *(They are not necessarily history; they are designed primarily to tell some important truth.)*

2. What do they remember about the book of Psalms? *(There are many different kinds of psalms: thanksgiving, praise, laments, messianic.)*

3. What is the Song of Solomon about? *(It is an allegory about the love of God for his people, or actual love poetry about man and woman and God's blessings on them.)*

4. What do the wisdom writings have in common? *(They are all efforts to use the mind God has given us to understand the world we live in.)*

5. What are the two main kinds of wisdom? *(commonsense sayings like the Proverbs, and wisdom that recognizes the disappointments in life).*

6. What important thing about human responses to God did we learn from this chapter? *(honesty).*

It might be a good idea to collect the writings of the class into a book. This book could be decorated and put together by the class during the remainder of the hour. It should be saved, either for sharing at a family night or for a display where the congregation can see what has been written.

Closing prayer

Ask several students to lead in closing prayer. They might want to use something written by students earlier.

Home assignment

Ask the students to read Chapter 16 of the reading book and the Bible passages from Daniel. Also suggest that they talk in their family about the end of the world. When and how will it come? What do the various members think about this? Why do they feel the way they do? They should write a paragraph about this in their notebooks for sharing with the class next time.

Remember that you are close to completing the first half of this year's material. This is the time to think about whether you wish to share the material in some way with the congregation, especially the parents and families of your class members.

If you wish to give an exam, announce it this week so that your students will have two weeks to review and prepare for it.

If you wish to share what has been studied with others, consider holding a family night or open house for your class and their parents. Perhaps you want to give this option consideration in class, allowing the students to decide how they can best share what they have experienced.

You could ask students to bring their notebooks and to set up displays of their creative projects. A brief review could be given by various students, touching highlights of each Old Testament chapter. It could be a time for becoming reacquainted with parents and also for renewing each family's commitment to grow together. Each parent could be introduced and a social time provided. This would enable you to meet anyone who has special questions or comments, and to express the hope for continued support from home in the next semester's study.

Be sure that written word goes to each home with details about the sharing night in time to allow parents to make plans to join you. The best time for this would be after you study Chapter 16 or if you give an exam, after the exam week.

The Time Between

Objective
The objective of this lesson is to acquaint the student with the period of time between the Old and New Testaments. This lesson is a link between our study of the Old and the New, and serves to set the stage for the coming of Jesus.

Biblical basis
Daniel 7:1-14; 12:1-13

Background information
This chapter is the connecting link which enables us to move from Old Testament history into the New Testament story of Christ and his followers.

This intertestamental period covers the years from 350 B.C. to the time of Jesus. It is a difficult time to study because of the lack of sources. You might want to consult a Bible dictionary for further background.

Our reading book mentions the name of Josephus. He was a Jewish historian around the end of the first century after Christ, and his works are a principal source of Jewish history at this time.

Also, the reading book uses the terms *apocrypha* and *apocalyptic*. The word *apocrypha* in the Greek means "hidden books." It was applied at first as a term of honor, since they were books supposedly containing hidden wisdom. But then the word came to mean "spurious" or "heretical" because it was believed these books contained harmful teachings. Today the word refers to a group of religious books which were written during the last two centuries B.C. and the first century after Christ. They are valuable sources of information for our understanding of the history, culture, and religion of Judaism, and contain background for the New Testament, but they are not usually included in our Bible.

Those writings termed *apocalyptic* have a dualistic feature about them that says (1) the world is evil, or at least evil forces are in control of it and it is in bad shape; and (2) God is good, and he will fight the powers of evil himself. The apocalyptic writings make much of (1) *eschatology*, which is talk about the end of the world coming soon; (2) *symbolism*, which means the use of images, particularly animals or beasts which are part of a code language for the characters they represent; and (3) *numbers*, which have a mystical significance in predicting when things will take place. Both the book of Daniel and the book of Revelation contain apocalyptic writing.

Preparation for class
You may want to review a little of the historical setting before teaching this lesson. Alexander the Great had conquered the world, so that the Jews were under Greek control and influence. About 250 B.C., the Old Testament began to be translated into Greek. This was the Bible used by the early Christians. Later, the New Testament was also written in Greek. Eventually Greek thought permeated every area of life.

If you can display a map of the world at this time, your class will get an idea of the extent of Greek conquest and influence. After Alexander died, his kingdom was split and eventually this led to the rebellion of the Maccabees described in the reading book. Carefully read the chapter and the biblical material related to it.

The lesson experience
Open the class with a brief overview of where we've been, using the time line. Mention a few of the highlights of the Old Testament story.

Remind your class that this lesson is a bit different in that what we know about this time comes from sources other than the Bible. A map of the world of Alexander the Great would be a help in showing how the world was divided and governed at this time. This could serve as an introduction to Greek influence. You may want them to use a summary of the following highlights for their notebooks:

1. *Alexander the Great.* During the intertestamental period he ruled the world and influenced everything from philosophy to architecture with his Greek ideas. His method was to allow defeated people a good deal of freedom to run their own lives, so being under his control wasn't all that bad. But after he died, it was a different story.

2. *The Greek language.* Point out that during this time it became common for Jews to speak Greek, rather than their own Hebrew language. About 250 B.C., the Old Testament began to be translated into Greek. This became the Bible for early Christians; the New Testament was written in Greek.

3. *The rebellion of the Maccabees.* This came about when Alexander died. At first, Palestine was controlled by those in Egypt, then control of Palestine shifted to Syria, and there was less and less freedom. The inability to run their own affairs and worship as they chose frustrated the Jews. When Antiochus forced the Jews to do things that were condemned by their religion, there was rebellion. It was led by Judas Maccabeus whose guerilla type of warfare was very effective.

4. *The beginning of the Roman influence.* From about 63 B.C., Judea was under the evil King Herod, who was a puppet of the Romans. He was ruler for about 30 years and knew how to please the Romans in order to stay in power. He did much to earn his reputation as a ruthless murderer. He was the one who had all the male babies murdered at the time of Jesus' birth.

5. *The Apocrypha.* Here is your opportunity to explain a little about these books. Place the word on the board and repeat it several times since it's a bit of a tongue-twister. Review what the chapter says about these writings and why they are important. If possible, bring a Roman Catholic edition of the Bible so you can show them the apocryphal books. As Protestants, we have made the same choice as the Jews and accepted these books as helpful, but not of the same stature and importance as those generally accepted and included in Holy Scripture.

6. *Apocalyptic writing.* Write this word on the board, and in explaining it, use it over and over. Have the students heard it before? Have they used the word apocalypse, or seen any references to it? What images and words flash into mind when it is spoken? If some of them have information, let them share it. Ask your students how this term is defined in the reading book.

If there is time, read the passages in Daniel and look briefly in the book of Revelation in the New Testament. Point out that this writing comes out of a time of great crisis and danger.

How do you survive in such a world? The people living in the intertestamental period had a variety of opinions about how to survive and how the world should be run. Some people decided to compromise. To them, it seemed a good idea to play the game of getting along. They made the best deal they could and settled for keeping silent and doing what they were told.

Another solution to the problem was to seek isolation. Some just decided to keep the law, wait for God to do something, and stay clear of worldly conflict. A more extreme position of this kind was taken by those who actually packed up and left. They formed communities where they could live with others who thought as they did and expected the end of the world shortly.

At the other extreme were the fighters. They wanted to get rid of the Roman authority, set up their own government, and start over. They saw themselves as soldiers and crusaders in a holy war.

Can your students recognize any of these types in our world today? Do they know people who fit into these categories? Talk about the reactions people have to world problems and life situations today. How does one go about choosing what is the best thing to do? Would they be interested in life in a commune? Do they want to compromise and blend in with the scenery? Are they interested in fighting the establishment?

Whatever we do, God is there. This is the kind of world Jesus came to. There were a million needs—and that many ideas as to what God should do about them. God had his own idea of what to do. He sent his son, Jesus, to be the answer.

Summary quiz. You may wish to give the class a quiz such as the following on Chapters 14–16. Let students correct them in class.

1. Name one important accomplishment during the period after the return from exile *(rebuilding the temple, beginning the Bible collection, returning to the land)*.

2. Name one of the problems during this time *(isolation, legalism, disappointment)*.

3. Name one book of the Old Testament which covers one of these problems and what to do about it *(Jonah, Ruth)*.

4. Name two of the three categories of writing in the Old Testament besides the story we've been following *(story, song, wisdom)*.

5. Name one book of the Bible that is an example of human response to God *(Psalms, Job, Song of Solomon)*.

6. Name two different kinds of psalms *(lament, praise, thanksgiving, messianic)*.

7. What do the wisdom writings have in common? *(They are all efforts to use the mind God has given us to understand the world we live in)*.

8. Who was the most influential world leader during the intertestamental period? *(Alexander the Great)*.

9. What is the name given to books written at this time which are included in the Roman Catholic Bible but not in the Protestant or Jewish Scriptures? *(Apocrypha)*.

10. What book of the Bible included much talk about the end of the world? *(Daniel, Revelation)*.

Closing prayer

This might be a good time for a "popcorn" prayer about our own needs and God's ability to meet those needs with what is best for us.

Home assignment

Can you believe that we are already halfway through our course? It has been an exciting story, full of action. This is a good time to evaluate. You could take questions from the quizzes in this guide, or write your own test, or maybe you'd like the students to write a test. But it is important to spend some time in written or oral evaluation of what has happened during these past 16 weeks.

If you choose not to give a test, consider asking each student to write a brief paper about the material covered in these first 16 lessons. It could be two to four pages in length and highlight the story of God and his people in the Old Testament. This is their opportunity to say what they think about the book, the class, and the methods we're using to learn together and build relationships.

The suggestion was made in the last lesson to consider a family night or open house for the congregation, or at least for the parents and families of your class. If you do this, here are several possibilities you might want to consider:

1. Set up a display of projects and creative activities that will interest visitors in what you have studied.

2. Communicate to visitors what has happened. Students could describe the projects or the various chapters, and thus share where they have been this semester.

3. Demonstrate your methods by using a short dramatization, a taped interview, role playing or skits. Let the students plan and produce these themselves.

4. Be sure to thank the parents for their support and solicit their continued prayers and cooperation. Give them some hints on ways in which they can be helpful, and encourage them to participate by showing interest at home.

5. Celebrate your class. Let both parents and students know how much you have enjoyed the class, and how you look forward to more good times. The open house or family night could be held during class time if you will have enough class sessions to complete the 32 lessons in this course, or on a Sunday afternoon or some evening. Be sure to publicize it and communicate by written or oral means with those you wish to invite.

If you plan to begin the first New Testament lesson during your next session, ask them to read that lesson in preparation for class.

Personal evaluation

It may be good at this point to take a few minutes and look at where we've been, how we got here, and where we're headed. Consider these questions:

- How did you feel about the class at the beginning of the year?
- Do you feel you've grown together as a group? Is it a group whose members care about each other? What kinds of things happen that you really like?
- How do you feel about the objectives you had in mind for the group? For the material? Does it seem that good things are happening with the lessons? Where do things get bogged down?
- Are the lessons flowing together into a story as you intended them to? Do you think the students understand the basic structure of the Old Testament?
- What do you seem to do best? What things are hardest for you to do? Can you think of other approaches or people who might be able to help with these things?

Don't be too hard on yourself. Remember we are learning together. We live under a gospel of love and grace. Take a deep breath—relax—and focus on the coming lessons.

The Old Testament Period

	Biblical era	Leaders	Prophets	World powers
2000 B.C.				
	Patriarchs	Abraham		
		Isaac		
		Jacob		
		Joseph		
1300				
	Exodus	Moses		Egypt / Assyria
		Aaron		
1200		Joshua		
	Judges	Ehud		
		Jephthah		
1100		Deborah		
		Gideon		
		Samson	Samuel	
1000	United Kingdom (1020-922)	Saul		
		David	Nathan	
		Solomon		
900	Divided Kingdom (922-722)	11 kings in Judah	Elijah	
			Elisha	Syria
		19 kings in Israel		
800			Amos	
			Hosea	
			Isaiah	Assyria
			Micah	
	Judah alone (722-587)	9 kings including Josiah		
700				
			Zephaniah	
			Nahum	
			Jeremiah	Babylon
			Habbakuk	
600				
			Ezekiel	
			Obadiah	Persia
	Exile and return		Haggai	
500		Nehemiah	Joel	
		Ezra	Zechariah	
			Malachi	
400	Inter-testamental period			Greece
		Maccabees	Daniel	Jewish independence
100				
A.D.				Rome

Time Lines

```
B.C.  2000
      1900
      1800    Patriarchs
                  Abraham
      1700        Isaac
                  Jacob
      1600        Joseph
      1500
      1400
      1300    Exodus from Egypt
      1200    Conquest
      1100    Period of the judges
      1000    United monarchy
                  Saul, David, Solomon
       900        Solomon dies   922
              Israel and Judah   922-722
       800        Elijah about 850
                  First writing prophets   after 750
       700    Kingdom of Judah   722-587
                  Jerusalem falls   587
       600
              Babylonian exile
       500
              Resettlement under Persian rule
       400        Rebuilding of temple
       300    Intertestamental period
                  Maccabean revolt   168
       200
       100    Roman supremacy

                  BIRTH OF CHRIST
                  Jerusalem destroyed   70
A.D.   100
```

| ministry of Jesus | the story of Jesus is told | Paul writes his letters | the four gospels are written | the book of Revelation is written |

A.D. 27-30   50   65   90   100

The Story of God's Love

Part 2

If a new teacher is taking over for the New Testament portion of this course, it is important that he or she read the introduction of this teacher's guide, beginning on page 3. If the same teacher is continuing, it would still be a valuable reminder of what this course is about.

Remember that you are not expected to do everything in this guide. There are more activities suggested than anyone could carry out. Read the entire lesson; then pick the activities that you have time for and that will work best in your situation.

Objective
The objective of this chapter is to make the transition from the Old Testament story of God and his people to the New Testament story of the fulfillment that comes in Jesus Christ.

Background information
The previous lessons have dealt with the Old Testament story of God's people, beginning with Abraham. For the most part we have followed a historical sequence of persons and events. Our theme has been God's unfailing love for his people and his continuing promises to them.

It is harder to maintain a historical sequence in the New Testament. It deals more with the event of the cross and resurrection. Jesus and his work is the central theme and everything else is secondary. So the chapters dealing with this New Testament material relate more to *subjects* than to *time*.

Remember that there is a gap between the time of Jesus and the time of the writing of the gospels. We should keep this in mind as we study the New Testament because it gives us a perspective in interpreting what the gospels intend to say.

Preparation for class
You will need to spend some time thinking of ways in which you can briefly review the major events and people of the Old Testament in order to introduce the New Testament. The idea you want to communicate is that there is one continuing story throughout the Bible: God loves his people, and that love includes us. In your review, help your students see the continuity in Old Testament events, but also the continuity between Old and New Testaments. The one thread which runs through the whole story is that God loves us. He sticks with us and calls us his own. And no matter what we do, he continues to love and care for us, and promises us life with him.

The lesson experience
Bring a ball of red yarn to class with you. As your students arrive, ask each one to hold on to the ball as you unwind it. You hang on to the end of the string. Pass the ball on to each student as he or she arrives. No one lets go of the yarn, though! As the ball is passed from person to person, everyone should continue to hold the yarn at the point they unwound it from the ball.

When everyone has arrived and is a part of the continuous length of yarn, begin asking questions: Think of this yarn as a story. Where is the beginning? How do we find its ending? What might each person in the class represent in the "long yarn" we're telling? Why should each person continue to hold his spot on the yarn? What would happen to the story if one person let go? How would it affect the person? Would it make a difference in the story?

Then move to the story line idea in the Bible. The study we have just made of the stories of the Old Testament has many parts. Who are some of the people they remember? *(Abraham, David, Solomon, Moses, Isaiah, Jeremiah).* Suppose these characters were in the places the students are in now. Imagine each of them as a person in a continuous story—each one only a chapter in a single, long serial. What would they call the story? How would it end? Is the end of the Old Testament the end of the story? Our lesson this week is about picking up that red thread of the story, and telling the best part!

At this point, collect the yarn and ask the students to turn to Chapter 17, the first chapter in the second part of their student book. Give them a few minutes to review what is written there. Go back to the question of what the story of the Old Testament might be called. Ask the students to write one-line titles for it in their notebook. Then share with everyone the various ideas.

Reread the paragraph on page 105 in the student book that begins, "God likes people. That is what the story has really been saying." Have the class take another look at their titles and pick out those that fit this description of the story.

What's in the New Testament. Turn to the table of contents in your Bibles and talk about some of the kinds of books found in both the Old and New Testaments. Count the books in each and see that there are 39 and 27 books, respectively. Point out that the Bible is like a small library, but all the books are really telling that one story.

Recall the kinds of books we found in the Old Testament. On the board list words like *history, poetry, songs, stories,* and *laws.* Then ask what kinds of books we can expect to find in the New Testament. Let them use their student books to help you list on the board: four gospels that tell the story of Jesus and his ministry; a book of history that describes the acts of the apostles; 21 books which are letters written to early Christian congregations and people; and finally a book that deals with a spectacular revelation. As you write this on the board, have your students record it in their notebooks.

Ask why the New Testament doesn't simply pick up the story from the Old Testament where it left off? The answer is that most of Jesus' contemporaries did not accept him as the leader God had sent to save them. To us it seems impossible that they didn't accept Jesus as the Savior. But remember these people had other ideas of what the Messiah would be like. Some were looking for a great king, others for a prophet, still others for a high priest. And some thought God would destroy the world completely, and only a faithful few would be left to make a fresh start.

Even today people have a variety of expectations about Jesus. What do you want Jesus to be? If you were looking for someone to save the world today, what type of person would it be? Does Jesus meet what you are looking for in a Savior? Was he the answer for the people of the Old Testament? Have your students answer these questions in their notebooks.

What comes first? Look at the table of contents in your Bibles again. Ask your students what they think are the most important books of the New Testament. Why did they choose certain books? Point out that the four gospels tell the story! But the gospels were written *after* many of the other books. Then, why are they first in the New Testament? They are first because they contain the heart of the story—the life and ministry of Jesus.

But the gospels don't tell us everything. Each of these writers was sorting through a large number of accounts, using what fit the needs of his audience. Some of the things we find there fit our needs, and some are of less direct value to us, but may have been important when written. Ask your students what are some of the things they would like to know that are not included in the gospels? List their ideas on the board. Some questions people have suggested they'd like answered are: Was Jesus married? What did he look like? What kind of family upbringing did he have? How did he treat his brothers?

Help your class see that the writers were interested in telling what they felt was most important. They emphasized the events that showed most clearly that Jesus is the one God sent. Each writer had a slightly different idea as to exactly what was important. Each wrote to different people. Some relied on the writings of others, but each told the story in his own way.

Although there are differences in the telling of the story, it's still the same story. What are some of the advantages of having four gospels written by four different people? Help your students to see that these four accounts of the story of Jesus give us a more complete picture of Jesus and his work. List the following ideas on the board and at the same time have your class write them in their notebooks. Your students may want to include additional ideas.

1. Each gospel writer wrote in his own way, from his own viewpoint.

2. Each writer was addressing himself to different people, just as we are all different.

3. Details left out by one are often filled in by another; one story overlooked completely might be included by another writer.

Close this discussion by asking your students to read the last page of the chapter again and tell in one sentence what they think is the most important idea of the Gospels. Discuss their ideas and get them included in their notebooks. The purpose of this closing is to get the students to focus once again on the theme that this is the story of God's love for his people—and we are included in that love because we are his people, too.

Closing prayer

Prayer by one of the students could close the session. Continue to emphasize the idea that the story of Jesus and his ministry is the fulfillment of the Old Testament story of God and his promises to his people. Now Jesus is center stage.

Home assignment

Ask the class to read all of Chapter 18 of the student book to prepare for next week's class. If you are planning to make a field trip or to invite guest speakers for next week on the chapter about Jesus' death, announce it now and give any directions that might be needed. Make your arrangements ahead of time and give your class instructions on where to meet and anything else they might need to know.

Death to King Jesus!

18

Objective

The purpose of this lesson is to point to the death of Jesus on the cross as central in our story of God and his people. Death in all of its brokenness is present in our world, but God is present, too, and he has the final word.

Biblical basis

Isaiah 53; Luke 22:14—23:56

Background information

It is important to keep in mind a number of things when we begin working on these New Testament chapters. It might help to point out that most studies have told the story of Jesus' life from a different perspective, beginning with his life and ending with his death. We begin with the cross because this is the central event from which all of his life and ministry take on meaning. The issue of death and the power of God over life and death are what Jesus Christ is all about.

All of us are aware of death. Each student will be able to identify with the idea that everyone will die. Death is final and ultimate. Jesus' death and his power over death can be central in identifying him as God's King. Even death takes on a new significance when we understand that God can use it and that he has defeated it.

Try to be comfortable with the subject of death. You should be able to discuss it with your class. Various opinions about it will come out and all kinds of questions will be raised. Allow some freedom and some levity. Remember that humor and fear are often closely connected. We may find class members making light of death and dying rather than facing their own fears about it. You can help them see death as a reality and also see beyond it—God is in charge even here.

Be careful not to go too far in this chapter, since the next chapter will deal with resurrection. Also, it's easy to get sidetracked in areas of unanswered questions about death. Some of this is necessary in order to stimulate our thinking about the experience, but it can lead to a circle of questions which have no answers.

Preparation for class

There are a number of directions that you can go in dealing with this chapter. There is certainly plenty of material to occupy you for an entire class period. There is also the opportunity of making use of a number of outside resources.

1. Your pastor might be a person who could talk with you about people's reactions to death. He might come and share some ideas about his experiences with dying people and funeral practices, and at the same time answer questions the students might have.

2. Or a local funeral director might be helpful in communicating with the students about death and its meaning. Visiting a funeral home would help them face the reality of death as a basic fact of our broken world. Maybe you would want to invite your pastor to come along.

3. Or consider a panel—someone who has lost a loved one and is able to share the experience, a pastor, a funeral director, and anyone else who could help build understanding about death.

Using resource people, or visiting a funeral home could take most of your class time. This is perfectly all right. But always prepare for a visit or special guests by having your students write questions in advance that help zero in on the issues of the chapter. This will help your resource people to know what it is you are expecting from them and also give a structure for the time you will spend with them. Explain to your resource people what is in the chapter and also the main issues you are interested in discussing.

The lesson experience

How you begin this lesson depends on which options you have chosen. If you will spend most of your time outside the classroom, begin with a brief introduction about where you are going and why, using the reading book chapter as the basis.

If you will be in the classroom, introduce any special guests or prepare your class for their arrival by explaining who they are and why they will be involved in this week's lesson. Then you can proceed with the class plan included here.

Remember the ball of red yarn that the class used last week? Bring it to class again. This time attach one end at the farthest point on your bulletin board or chalkboard. Unwind the yarn to stretch the full length of the board. Leave the ball on the end, but secure it to the board with a pin. Then make a story line of the yarn. Ask the class to quickly recall key events or people that might be called a part of the red thread that is the story of God and his people. What would they consider the starting point? Creation? Or Abraham? See how many names and events they can remember. Place a pin or piece of tape with the name or event on it along the yarn as they remember. Try to use only about one-half of the yarn to cover the entire Old Testament period.

Remind your class that last week we read that the story of the Old Testament had some great people in it. God loves people. These stories might have ended with the words "to be continued." The books of the New Testament tell the continued story of God and his people. Today we'll see that there is a main character or hero in this part of the story. But he is a different kind of hero. Our story is about Jesus—a cross—and death. This is the turning point in the story. Place a large pin or a cross at the midpoint on the yarn.

As Christians we consider the cross of Jesus to be central to our story of God's love for his people. This is why the event is placed in the center position on the red thread. Many things lead up to this story and many things refer back to it later. Death is the proof of the broken nature of man in this world, but God's love in Jesus Christ is the answer to this brokenness.

Take a look at the chapter. Leave the red thread pinned to the board and turn to the reading book. Give your class a few minutes to review what they read about death. Then begin by asking what they thought about the chapter. Do they agree that everybody is going to die? Do they find it morbid or fearful to read that they, too, are headed for the grave? You'll probably find that some young people do not want to talk about dying at all, or can only handle it with nervous humor.

Ask, "Why do people die?" Help them to restate what we learned in our study of the Garden of Eden about man's decision to disobey God and the consequences of that choice. We don't die because of heart failure, or because we stop breathing, or because of old age. Those things are symptoms of the real problem, which is the broken relationship with God. Other things resulted from the decision to disobey such as pain, the drudgery of work, and expulsion from the garden, but the fundamental and most real example of the brokenness is death.

The next question is, "What is God doing about it?" Isn't the fact that we all die evidence that God has deserted us—that he has finally given up? The story this week says he has done just the opposite.

The emphasis in our next lesson is on the resurrection. Easter brings back echoes of the Old Testament prophecies. God won after all—even over death. But this week we want to take time to study Jesus' death and our own and see it as that "last enemy" to be destroyed.

At this point, carefully study the passages from Isaiah 53 and Luke 22–23. Have your class actually look them up in the Bible. Have them put these passages in their own words in their notebooks so they can fully realize the impact of both the prophecy and the fulfillment. They should do this together, with your help. You may want to put some of their insights about prophecy and its fulfillment on the board.

What about us? Then ask what all this has to do with us? Does Jesus' death mean anything for us and our own involvement in death? Does it answer any important questions we might have about death? Questions such as these:
1. Will I die too?
2. Is it all right to fear death?
3. How should I feel about dying?
4. How do I feel about funerals?

There may be other questions that you or the class want to add. But help them to face the reality of death—to see it as that fundamental experience of brokenness—but also to see that God is in control of the situation. We can't answer all the questions about it, but we do know something important—Jesus went through it for us and made it possible for us to conquer death also.

Writing your will. If there is time, an optional project would be to have your students write their own wills. Most of us put off such things as being morbid, but a Christian can face death from a different perspective.

Ask your students to take out their notebooks and title a page *Last Will and Testament*. Ask them to write a will concerning what they would want given to their survivors if they should die. Are there people they want to thank? Are there special possessions they want given to certain people? Something special they wish to say to someone they love? What would they write as the last thing they might be remembered saying?

Happy ending. The importance of this story is that it has a happy ending. This week we want to emphasize the reality of death for both Jesus and us. But next week we want to emphasize the triumph of Jesus in the resurrection. Prepare your class for next week's study by using the last few minutes to talk about questions that death raises. Many of these take on new meaning for us when we see them in the light of the resurrection.

Closing prayer

This lesson requires that we be aware of our students and their special needs. By this time you will know more about your students and their families. Are there those who have recently suffered a loss through the death of a parent or other family member? Be open to expressions, either verbal or through gestures, which show anxiety, fear, or grief. You might be able to help these young persons express their emotions or you might approach them later with a special word of comfort.

This lesson could be a hard one for young people who have doubts and fears about death. End the class with the assurance that God's people have hope. Lead a prayer in a positive and thankful way, praising God for the hope that is ours in Jesus Christ.

Home assignment

All students should read Chapter 19 for next week. They should also write a paragraph in their notebooks about what Jesus' resurrection story tells us about death and life.

Long Live King Jesus!

19

Objective

The purpose of this lesson is to show that in Jesus' resurrection we have victory over the power of evil in the world. The death of Jesus is not the end—his resurrection declares that God has overcome all opposition. We are all participants in this victory because Jesus is God's promise to us.

Biblical basis

Luke 24:1-53

Background information

In preparing for this class, you should carefully study Luke 24 and 1 Corinthians 15. Do not worry about having adequate answers to the questions your class raised at the end of the last session, or the ones that may present themselves this week. There are many things for which we do not have the answers. It is important for you to establish that it's all right to have questions and it's also all right to not always have the answers. If you feel uncomfortable with some of the questions, perhaps your pastor can be a resource for you.

Preparation for class

This is a story that is often told. Make an effort to have a number of good resources to use in this session. Check your church's film and filmstrip library for a good review of the resurrection story and the days following Easter. This would be a way of helping your class to visualize what happened.

Religious art that deals with the topics of the crucifixion and the resurrection is plentiful. Collect a number of art pieces from around the church or community, or use several pictures of art work dealing with this theme. If you want to encourage your students to paint or draw or make symbols, bring the needed materials to class along with sheets of paper or tagboard.

The lesson experience

Why not open with prayer? Ask one of the students to begin and two or three others to add their own ideas. End the prayer yourself with words of thanks for God's great gift of Jesus and his Easter victory.

Review the events of the past two lessons. Can the students verbalize or put into words the main point of last week's lesson? What was the center point of the red thread? How does the cross relate to my life? Be sure to have your students read some of the paragraphs they were assigned to write last week.

Give the class a few minutes to reread Chapter 19 and Luke 24. Before they begin, tell them we plan to look more closely at the resurrection and events following it to see what it teaches us about our own death and resurrection.

A film or filmstrip would fit well at this point. If you are using one, make sure it is set up and ready to go. Ask your students to watch the various characters in these events to note their reactions to what is happening. How would they describe the reactions? Can they see themselves in this situation? What would they have done? What would they have asked? Doesn't it seem odd that the disciples had been told by Jesus that these things would happen—and they were still taken by surprise? Why was this?

A taped narrative. The idea of this exercise is to help the students put themselves into the roles of the people involved in the resurrection.

Assign roles to various people. Possible characters would be the narrator (or on-the-street interviewer), the women at the tomb, the angel, the two disciples on the road to Emmaus, uninvolved onlookers. Remind those taking part that they are to reconstruct that day as though it were today with themselves as the participants. They should refer to Chapter 19 and Luke 24 for help. Then each should write a brief summary of what the character represented would say if questioned about what happened. The interviewer can draw up some questions for a news program in which people who were there are interviewed. Allow some time for practicing the roles. Students may want background music or noise to help make the narrative authentic.

When everyone is ready, tape the narrative as though it were a live news show—an on-the-spot report of the resurrection. Encourage each person to be as expressive as possible, adding details and human interest angles. Students should try to be conscious of how the people felt, what happened to them inside, what they did, thought, and remembered—and how it changed their viewpoint. Once the interview is finished, the class will be anxious to have you play the tape.

An example of possible dialog:

Interviewer: We're at the garden belonging to Joseph. There's been a report this morning of some strange happenings here. We have with us a woman who claims to have talked with an angel. Now, ma'am, can you tell us in your own words just what you did see?

Mary: I saw an angel! I tell you it was a messenger of God! I—or rather we, came to the grave—and the body was gone! I mean, it wasn't stolen or anything—it's just gone! I can't believe it! There were two men who talked to us—not like ordinary men—they looked like angels. . . .

This experience could be a good way to get the students thinking about the mysterious nature of the resurrected Jesus. They would have had some chance to "feel" with people about what Jesus said and did after he was raised from the dead. Suggest to them that we look into the idea of what he was like, how people came to know him, and what all this means to us.

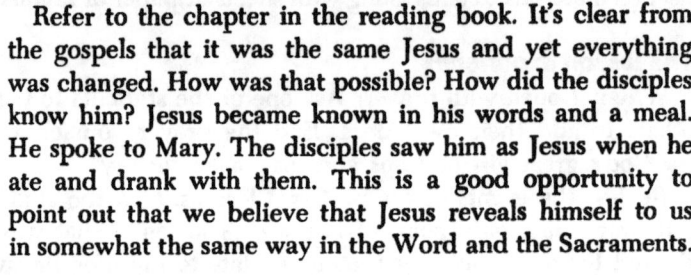

Refer to the chapter in the reading book. It's clear from the gospels that it was the same Jesus and yet everything was changed. How was that possible? How did the disciples know him? Jesus became known in his words and a meal. He spoke to Mary. The disciples saw him as Jesus when he ate and drank with them. This is a good opportunity to point out that we believe that Jesus reveals himself to us in somewhat the same way in the Word and the Sacraments.

You may want the students to write in their notebooks a sentence or two about the resurrected body and the way Jesus reveals himself to his followers. If you have invited the pastor, this is an excellent time for asking him questions about the resurrected body and our own practices and beliefs.

Religious art can also be used in several ways at this point. If there is little time or if you choose not to do an art project, you could still collect some pictures and display them around the room as visual interpretations of the resurrection. Give the students several minutes to browse and comment on various artists' concepts of the resurrection.

If you want to do a project, use the art as an introduction to the students' doing their own works of art. Discuss the impressions the art objects give. Can the students think of symbols they have seen in the church or elsewhere that represent resurrection? Or can they develop new symbols? Some examples of symbols are the butterfly, flowers, the egg, sunrise and sunset, and the seasons. Compare these symbols with Luke's description of the resurrection.

Encourage your class to draw, color, or paint to depict in some way their feelings about the resurrection. They don't have to draw Jesus, though they may if they like. They might focus on the reactions of one person who saw Jesus—or one place involved—or choose to do symbols that have meaning for them—or their own reaction to the idea of resurrection. It should be an attempt to put into art their personal involvement in the idea of Jesus and resurrection. What does it mean for them?

Allow time for thinking and reworking ideas, and then for actually drawing or painting. Try to go around the room giving individual help and encouragement. The idea is for each person to really express himself or herself. Be supportive of individual efforts.

Sharing these art pieces could be done in a number of ways. You could set up a display, asking each student to write a short paragraph of explanation to go with his art piece. You could have a sharing time in which each student tells about what has been done. Or this may be a time when the work is considered a private venture, shared only by those who volunteer.

In conclusion. But what happens now? At the end of the lesson, try to find time to deal with these points:

1. Jesus doesn't leave his disciples alone; he promises his Spirit to give them power for telling others about him. We have that same kind of promise, that same power, and that same mission.

2. Jesus has done it all—he came to tell us that God forgives us. He faced death so people would know God is in charge. He has taken care of everything.

3. Jesus is not the end of the work God had been doing all along and continues to do among people. The story is far from over. The world still has pain, sorrow, sin, and death. The turning point has been passed but there is still a job to do! Those of us who know the story have a mission to tell it to others.

We will get into the idea of the commissioning of the disciples in the Pentecost story, but here is your chance to introduce the idea that all of us have been chosen to pass along the word that God is in charge. Jesus is real. God's kingdom is forever.

Home assignment

Ask the students to read Chapter 20 for next week and to write a short paragraph describing John the Baptist in their own words. Encourage them to dare to be imaginative in what they do. You might also want to have a short test over the first three chapters of our New Testament study.

20

Get Ready for the Kingdom

Objective
The purpose of this lesson is to point out that the ministry of Jesus began with his baptism by John who called people to repentance and forgiveness. The baptism of Jesus was a sign that the kingdom had come.

Biblical basis
Luke 3 and 4

Background information
Of the four gospels, our concentration will be upon the gospel of Luke during this New Testament study. It will be helpful to you to read the whole gospel and then reread the parts that pertain to each lesson as you go along.

The four gospel versions of the baptism of Jesus as they are found in the reading book may seem repetitious at first glance. The point of including them is that they help us to get a fuller picture of the baptism and also emphasize its importance in our understanding of Jesus and his ministry. John the Baptist is the link between the Old and New Testaments. In studying John, we emphasize again the continuity of all of Scripture.

Preparation for class
In this lesson you have another opportunity to tie the Old and New Testament together. Draw attention to the similarity between John the Baptist and the Old Testament prophets studied earlier. The gospel of Luke emphasizes the continuity of Scripture. You can see Isa. 61:1-2 repeated by Jesus in Luke 4:16-21, and Isa. 40:3-5 repeated by John in Luke 3:4-6. The two parts of Scripture are the one continuous story we're always talking about.

You might like to collect some pictures or symbols of John the Baptist, including contemporary pictures of people who might be considered John the Baptists in our day. Display them in the room and use them to introduce the discussion of what he was like, what people thought of him, and what he considered to be his role in life. Can you find things or pictures of things that might symbolize John?

To summarize the New Testament work done so far, you might plan to give the following quiz on Chapters 17–19.

1. What is the central event of the New Testament? *(the death and resurrection of Jesus).*

2. Why are the four gospels first in the New Testament? *(They tell the story of Jesus' life and ministry).*

3. How many books are there in the New Testament? *(27).*

4. Why is there death? *(It is the essential evidence of the brokenness of human life when we do not obey God.)*

5. Did Jesus really die? *(Scripture tells us he did).*

6. How should I feel about dying? *(God is in charge and he is with us).*

7. What's the central point of the resurrection story? *(God has overcome suffering of all kind—he is in charge and Jesus is victorious for us).*

8. What is one symbol we connect with the resurrection? *(butterfly, egg, flowers, spring, sunrise, the seasons).*

9. Why did Jesus leave and return to his Father in heaven? *(His work here was finished and he had prepared others to continue it).*

10. What event is the highlight of the whole story of God and his people? *(resurrection).*

The lesson experience
You may want to begin with the quiz and then give your students a few minutes to review the material in Chapter 20 and also the biblical reading which

is very important in this chapter. Ask for volunteers to read Luke 3 and 4 aloud to the class.

This would be the time to have them read their imaginative paragraphs about John the Baptist. How would they react if they came to church on Sunday and heard his message? Can they rephrase some of what he told the people to do (Luke 3:10-14) in terms of what he might tell people of today about sharing and taxes and being content with wages? John emphasized honesty. How would such an emphasis be accepted today? Why is John important? Why do all the gospels agree that Jesus' ministry didn't really begin until after he had been baptized by John? Many of these questions are answered in the reading book.

Discuss the opening paragraphs of Chapter 20 which discuss how the followers of Jesus tried to get going on the work they had to do after he left. They made mistakes. But they had some ideas about what Jesus would want them to do and they remembered what he had said and done. Two things were clear:

1. They wanted to show how the story of Jesus fit into the longer story of God and his people.

2. They knew that a disciple should try to be like the teacher—so they used memories, stories, personal experiences, and the Scriptures to help them be what they felt this king would want them to be like.

Moving on to the second division in Chapter 20, see if your students can help you list on the board some of the reasons for four different gospel accounts:

1. Memories were different.
2. Language wasn't always uniform.
3. The audience of each writer was a group with certain needs and ideas.
4. Time passed, and many stories were told and retold before being written down.

One thing we want to emphasize is that the four gospels agree that Jesus' ministry began after his baptism by John. Each version has its own way of telling what happened. Divide the class into four groups and assign one gospel account of the baptism to each group. Have them reread the one account they are assigned, asking these questions: Who seems to be the central character here? Who seems to be telling the story—or from whose perspective is it written? What special details are included—dialog, description, time, place? As a group, share what was learned from the comparative study. Draw four parallel columns on the board and help the groups to list some of the things they found in each account.

Why is John so important? How do your students answer this question? Can they recall anybody from the previous chapters who was like John? What was that person like? Jesus saw John as a great prophet. What similarities does he have with the Old Testament prophets we have studied? Are there similarities with Elijah and Nehemiah? Do you see any similarities between John and the early leader, Moses? Do they remember the repentance cycle in Chapter 11? Was John preaching the same message?

John is called the last prophet because a new age comes in God's dramatic action of sending Jesus Christ who fulfills all the earlier prophecies. Investigate Isa. 61:1-2 and Luke 4:16-21. What is Jesus saying? Also Isa. 40:3-5 and Luke 3:4-6. Who is John? What is his task?

What really happened in the baptism of Jesus? Certainly Jesus didn't need baptism in order to be forgiven. What really happened that day was that Jesus was set apart and marked as God's special servant. The Spirit in the form of a dove was sent to tell us that God's kingdom has come!

Review the story in Luke 4:16-30 that tells about Jesus in Nazareth. Its significance can easily be overlooked. Jesus is preaching in his hometown. At first he seems to be received well, but what happens as a result of his speaking? The people find he means business. The result is anger on the part of the people.

Could this happen today? Ask your students to use their imagination. What would happen if a native resident returned to talk before the town council or the congregation to tell them that they were all wrong? Suppose he were to tell them that they needed to repent—that big changes were necessary in order to right things with God. How would the town take it? How would your local congregation greet this message?

Would we be interested in hearing what he had to say? Or would we be more interested in getting him out of town?

Closing prayer

Here might be a chance to have the students verbalize what they see in this lesson about Jesus' calling us to be on his side, or about John's pointing to Jesus as the fulfillment of God's promises. Ask your class to write one sentence in their notebooks which they think is the point of today's lesson, and then a one sentence prayer about what this lesson might mean for them. Then call on three or four to close with their sentence prayers.

Home assignment

John calls men to repent and Jesus calls them to discipleship. Next week we talk about discipleship. Ask the students to read Chapter 21 for next week.

Follow Me

Objective

The purpose of this lesson is to introduce the students to the kind of discipleship to which Jesus called people when he said, "Follow me" and to consider how this might relate to our lives. The miracles are seen as signs that authenticate his work and convinced the disciples that Jesus was doing what only God could do.

Biblical basis

Luke 5:1—6:16

Background information

Why were the people hesitant to believe in Jesus and follow him? Why couldn't they see who Jesus was right away? One of the purposes of our session is to help the students understand the concerns of these people about following a prophet.

The second thrust of this lesson is to deal with the miracles. The miracle stories cause people to react in various ways. There are believers who accept miracles without any questions and there are skeptics who have questions, wondering what the miracles were and why they are included in this lesson. The miracles point to who Jesus is—he was doing what only God could do. They seem to be saying, "This man is the promised one."

You can explore the miracles we are looking at in detail, and the lesson plan will give you suggestions for helping students to see and feel with the people of that time what was actually taking place.

The first two references in Chapter 21 are from an ancient book by Josephus. We met Josephus before in our work in the intertestamental period. He was a historian of early biblical times. You may want to study more about him in a good Bible dictionary or encyclopedia.

Josephus describes other leaders who made promises to the people, but ran up against the Roman government and proved themselves unequal to the opposition. The people who followed these men risked their lives—and some died for their devotion. When Jesus came on the scene, it was natural that many were hesitant to follow another leader with still another set of promises. They needed to know who he was; that's what the miracles are about.

Preparation for class

Plan your session in such a way that you can spend most of your time in small-group work. This will give you opportunities to look carefully into each of the four stories we are concerned with in this chapter. If your class is small, choose two or three stories and ask the class to work with them as one group; otherwise, divide your class into two or four groups and use all four stories.

Bring enough paper for writing role plays, letters, and newspaper articles. Be sure your students are bringing their Bibles each week to use in class. Depending on your group, if you want additional interest in the role plays, gather some clothing props for individuals to use in depicting these stories. Be sure to allow time to evaluate and discuss the stories.

The lesson experience

Write the words *Follow Me* in large print on your bulletin board or chalkboard. As you begin your class, ask the students to open their notebooks and write their definition of a miracle. Then have them share with a partner what they wrote and as a class talk a minute about miracles.

1. What do you think of when the word *miracle* is mentioned?
2. Who can perform miracles? Why?
3. Do you believe in miracles?

4. What is the relationship between Jesus and miracles?

Close the discussion with prayer, asking your students to contribute one sentence about their feelings concerning miracles and Jesus.

Discuss the means Jesus used to call disciples to follow him. The reading book reminds us that people were not always easily convinced. We can hardly blame them. There was good reason to be hesitant to believe.

Ask your class how they would recruit disciples. Would it be a preaching mission, a stadium and fanfare, or a tour of college campuses? Do they think Jesus had a plan in mind when he started his ministry? He seems to have stirred up trouble, especially with religious leaders. How do your students feel about this? How would they react to someone like Jesus? How would your congregation accept his style of ministry?

What are some measurements of the words of a prophet? The opening paragraphs of Chapter 21 suggest that we are to measure whether what he's saying goes along with the way he acts. And does what he's saying fit with the long story of God and his people. And finally, does he have anything to back up his words. This, of course, is where the miracles came in.

To study the evidence regarding Jesus' claims to be God's son, divide the class into four groups, assigning each group one of the four stories:
- The great catch of fish (Luke 5:1-11)
- The paralyzed man (Luke 5:17-26)
- The calling of Matthew or Levi (Luke 5:29-32)
- The Sabbath problems (Luke 5:29—6:11)

Suggest the following tasks for each group, explaining that they are to:

1. Read the Bible story again. Discuss what happened, why Jesus did what he did, and how you would react as part of this story.

2. Personalize it. That is, try to picture yourself as a participant in the event. Describe your feelings and the reactions to Jesus and those of others around you.

3. Retell the story in your words and be ready to share it with the class.

To add variety, each group should do something different with its story. Here are some ideas.

Group 1 could write a newspaper article about the great catch of fish. Describe what happened and people's reactions. Follow it up with personal information on Peter, James, and John. Choose a headline. Try to be interesting and factual, but with feelings included.

Group 2 could compose a letter as though it were written by the paralyzed man. Tell his story of affliction, what happened, who the onlookers were, and his own personal conviction about who Jesus is. It could be a letter to a friend or to parents, but include details and feelings.

Group 3 could dramatize the story of Levi and his decision to follow Jesus. Give parts to each member of the group and depict what happened to Levi, how others felt about his being among Jesus' followers, and how he changed.

Group 4 could simulate a church council meeting at which Jesus and his Sabbath habits were being discussed. Bring out the points that were made by the religious people in the story, what Jesus said and did, and how council members felt about these Sabbath problems.

Allow your students time to develop their ideas, dialog, costuming, art work, or whatever they want to include with their presentation. Encourage them to really put themselves into it.

Then share these retellings, giving each group an opportunity to make its presentation. Conclude by briefly discussing how the events we see in this chapter serve to authenticate who Jesus is—they are the evidence that God has sent him. He is doing what only God can do.

Ask your class how they would personally react to Jesus and his miracles. Many people in Jesus' time rejected him. They became the group who were out to get him. Others were convinced that he was the one they were looking for—nothing else mattered. They were ready to follow him, even if it meant leaving everything else behind.

If class time allows, pursue the "Son of man" concept. It begins in Old Testament prophecy and continues to come up in relation to Jesus again and again. Review what Chapter 21 says and read together the Old Testament prophecy in Daniel.

This Son of man was to be a judge and ruler. He was coming to bring forgiveness, but also punishment. Most people had the idea this would happen only at the end of the world. Now Jesus says he's bringing his kingdom right into the midst of the world. This was hard to accept, especially for religious people who had their own ideas about how God would do things.

If we were expecting this Son of man today, what would the class want him to do? What would they want him to be like? How would he relate to the problems of the world? What would he do about all the evil surrounding us? Encourage your class to express their thoughts about this.

For us today. Spend the last part of your period talking about how we follow Jesus today. Do the students feel Jesus has called them to follow him in the same way he called Levi? In what ways is our calling similar and in what ways is it different?

Discuss what it means to follow Jesus—does it mean we believe he does things that only God can do? What kinds of miracles do we have today? Following Jesus at the time when he lived was pretty risky business. Is this still true today? List some of the things that may be involved in following Jesus today. Does it mean forgetting about what the crowd says? Does it mean seeing Jesus as somebody special?

Next week we will be looking at Jesus' teaching methods and the content of his teaching. It will be another opportunity to study what is unique about Jesus and what it means to be his follower.

Home assignment

Ask the students to read Chapter 22 in the reading book for next week. Ask them to write two or three paragraphs about their best teacher. Who was it, why did they learn from that person, and how did the teaching happen?

22 Now Hear This!

Objective
The purpose of this lesson is to take a look at Jesus as a master teacher who taught more than moralisms. In his teaching, Jesus presents a God who reaches out to us where we are and as we are. In this lesson, we want to help students to better understand the fullness of God's love.

Biblical basis
Luke 6:17-49; 10:25-42; 15:1-32

Background information
Jesus was famous for the marvelous way in which he responded to people's questions. He often used stories or parables to get a point across. He seldom argued with people who sought to trap him, but often turned questions around so that the seeker had to answer it instead. As part of this class session, you will want to look at examples of his style of teaching and discuss them.

You will also want to help your students understand the extreme measures God is willing to take to win us over. God's love, as shown in the parables of the lost coin, the lost sheep, and the prodigal son, is overwhelming. Could it really be that he loves us that much and searches us out in our "lostness"? Jesus tells us exactly that. He teaches that God cares, and that he is willing to go to any lengths to make us his own.

Preparation for class
Collect some items that will help you portray the theme of being lost and being found. There are a number of traditional pictures which show the shepherd retrieving the lost sheep, the woman and the coin, or the prodigal son. You may have one of these pictures in your church or home which you could bring to class as a help in illustrating the theme of the lesson.

Another possibility is to visualize the Sermon on the Mount. Your students have heard about it, but probably never really looked at it. Write the Beatitudes on a large sheet of posterboard and use them as a focal point for discussing the straight talk Jesus used with his disciples concerning God's kingdom.

The lesson experience
Ask a student to open with prayer, or suggest a "popcorn" prayer from several class members. One student may begin by thanking God for things related to this week's lesson. In this case, suggest that your students consider the blessing of having good teachers and teaching materials. What specific things can they think of that God has given teachers which makes them fun and exciting to be around? Let the students think about this for a minute. This kind of prayer is spontaneous; short words or phrases "pop" in whenever anyone thinks of something to express. You could close the prayer.

Allow some time for your students to share their paragraphs about "my best teacher." As a result of this sharing, make up a list of the attributes of a good teacher. A student could be appointed to write the ideas on the board. Suggest that they share a word or phrase which describes a quality or characteristic in that person that made for good teaching.

Then share the list. Are words about personality mentioned, such as *friendly, warm, funny, understanding, kind, concerned*? What things were said which have to do with methods the teacher used? (*interesting, varied, involvement, different, relevant*).

Can they relate any of these things to what they have heard about Jesus as a teacher? Do they have any examples concerning how he taught and the kind of teacher he was? We read a number of stories about his teaching in this week's assignment. Keep these stories in mind as you make your comparisons.

Look at Chapter 22. Ask your students what there was about Jesus' teaching style that would lead us to conclude he was a good teacher. Help your students to see that everywhere he went, Jesus aroused interest in his teaching, as evidenced by the crowds. People listened carefully. They asked questions. Many made sacrifices in order to hear what he had to say. They even changed their lives on the basis of what he said—that takes quite a teacher!

Then look specifically at the kind of teaching Jesus did. Have your students write the word *parable* in their notebooks. Can they give some examples of parables? Can they come up with a simple definition of the word? These seemingly simple stories often had a deep and important meaning. At times it seemed almost like a secret which one had to discover for oneself. Why would Jesus use this kind of teaching tool? Reread Luke 10:25-42. How did Jesus get the lawyer to answer his own question? Why did Jesus do this?

Rather than being spoon-fed by the teacher, the learner himself must discover the point of a parable. Jesus in his teaching used questions in such a way as to allow learners to discover the answers for themselves.

Then turn to the Sermon on the Mount. If you have printed the Beatitudes on posterboard, draw attention to them now. Have they read and heard these words before? What have they heard about them? Do these words make any sense to them? What was Jesus talking about when he gave this sermon?

Make it clear that Jesus was talking about what it is like to be his disciple and to work in God's kingdom. Life for the followers of Jesus would not be a rose garden. What is Jesus saying in these Beatitudes? Do people turn to God more when they are in need, or when things are moving along smoothly? Who is supposed to be in control of life, according to Jesus? He describes the kingdom as something where God is in control.

The whole story of God's people shows this had to be learned again and again. Remember our Old Testament study—in times of plenty, people forgot God. When things got rough, they turned to God again, remembering the God who had promised to be with them. It was the same in Jesus' time.

How is it today? Can your students think of times when God seemed especially important to them? When does he seem to be forgotten? Jesus was telling his disciples that God will not abandon them no matter what happens. He still tells us this today.

Finally, help your students to see that in his teaching, Jesus communicated the gospel of God's grace. He conveyed the exciting and comforting truth that God loves us and that he will do anything to make us his own.

This is the time to make use of your art work. If you have been able to collect any pictures illustrating the parables, use them to introduce this section of the chapter. What is the artist picturing here? What do the facial expressions convey? What is the focal point of each picture?

Turn to Luke 15:1-32. Some of the religious leaders were complaining about the people Jesus hung around with. They criticized him for ignoring influential leaders and choosing for his followers people who seemed to be losers. Jesus tells the parables of the lost sheep, the lost coin, and the lost son as part of the answer to this criticism. He points out that God's central concern is for the one who is lost, and that God will go to any lengths to recover the one who is lost.

Talk about being lost. Has anyone in the class ever been lost? What were the circumstances? What feelings did the experience bring? Was it in a store, a new school, a new city? Another experience similar to this would be to feel left out in a group, or forgotten on a birthday or at a party. These kinds of experiences produce the anxiety and loneliness that being lost brings us.

Jesus' stories of being lost and found again bring so much joy because of their happy ending. We might expect that the shepherd would leave the one sheep and go home happy that he was able to keep so many of his flock together. The woman could have forgotten the lost coin and settled for looking later or running across it while cleaning some day. Instead she throws a party to celebrate finding that small amount.

Perhaps the best story is the one about the lost son. It points out that God is more than fair. This story would be excellent for role playing. If you have time in class, reread this parable. Then ask for volunteers to take the various roles in the parable. Suggest that they use their own words and update the story to a modern setting using short sentences. Then do the role playing and afterwards discuss how it applies to us.

Discuss the idea that God is our Father who pursues and loves us no matter how far away from him we stray. When we turn to him, he welcomes us as though we had never left. This is not always easy to understand for the brother who stays home. It doesn't seem fair—but God is more than fair, he loves us!

Students not involved in the role playing might want to do one of the following:

1. Try to write an ad for the personal column in a newspaper, describing something valuable that has been lost and what you will give for its return. What has to be considered in seeking to get the valuable back?

2. Write a letter home as though you were the lost son. Suppose you had left home and found out it didn't work. What things would you say in asking to come home? How would you describe what you felt and did, and what response would you expect from your parents?

3. Draw a symbol or picture about these parables of being lost. Can the students think of one or two things that describe or depict the idea of God and how he acts in these Bible stories? What color comes to mind when they think of being lost? What about being found?

Share and discuss the projects at the close of the lesson. Have them write some of the main points of the discussion in their notebooks and use them for a review in the next class session.

If you have not finished the Bible work in time to do the role-play, or if you prefer not to do the role-play for this session, you might want to consider using the record of Clarence Jordan's version of "The Good Samaritan and Other Parables." It is full of excellent insights and takes about 20 minutes to play.

Closing prayer

Ask the class to close with silent prayer. Some of the following phrases could be used as starters:
- Lord, when we get lost, thanks for finding us.
- Keep us on the right track and help us to listen when you have something to say to us.
- We're glad that you love us enough to look for us and to rejoice when we're around.
- Teach us to see others as you see us, valuable and important.
- Help us to see your kingdom is now.

Home assignment

Ask the students to read Chapter 23 for next week, including the biblical reading that is assigned in that chapter. For their notebooks, have them ask their parents who Martin Luther King was and write a paragraph on their response. Use their findings next week to introduce who Jesus is.

Who Do You Say that I Am?

Objective
The purpose of this lesson is to help the student to understand the mission of Jesus Christ, why this mission remained a secret to many while he was here on earth, and what it means for all of us that he was "the anointed one," "the Son of God."

Biblical basis
Luke 7:1-35; 9:7-36

Background information
It is important to allow the students the opportunity to personalize this lesson, that is, to ask themselves, "Who is Jesus?" in terms of their own relationship to him. You will need to strike a balance between the biblical narrative about who Jesus is and personal insight from your students about who Jesus is for each of them.

As background, it would be helpful to read the prolog in John 1:1-18 and Phil. 2:1-11. What terms are used to describe Jesus and his mission in these passages?

Remember that we are dealing primarily with the gospel of Luke. Luke stresses the continuity of the Old Testament promise of a Messiah and its fulfillment in Jesus. He is called "the Son of God," "the anointed one," "the King of kings," and more.

Study the biblical material in the chapter because it is basic to our theme of who Jesus was and what people thought about his mission. It also reminds us that this lesson is part of our long story of God and his people. You may want to review parts of our Old Testament study in talking about Jesus as God's promised Messiah. Remember Moses and Elijah and the expectations of the people of Israel for an "anointed one."

Preparation for class
Pictures of the transfiguration (Jesus with Moses, Elijah, and the sleepy disciples) or of John the Baptist could be used as discussion starters.

Creative writing or art work might be a way to personalize this week's study. Time needs to be given to deal with the important question of who Jesus is for each person in the class. Bring a variety of materials so that your students can choose between writing a poem or song about who Jesus is or doing some tempera painting about the subject. Encourage them to use their own ideas.

Jesus Christ Superstar has some good dialog about who Jesus is and what people thought about him. There is one lyric in particular which might be useful, where the disciples are asking Jesus, "Are you who they say you are? . . ." You could bring the record and play it as part of your session, asking students to think about what is being said and to discuss it.

The lesson experience
Before class, use a large strip of posterboard to write out the question, "Who do you say that I am?" Pin it across your bulletin board where everyone can see it as they come into the room. If you will be using pictures, hang them on the board, too.

Are there additional projects from the last class session that you can share as a way of review? Give your students a few minutes to review the reading in the chapter and the biblical material assigned within it.

Introduce the lesson by suggesting that for many years, people have wondered and argued about who Jesus is. The disciples themselves were often confused. Many people today have trouble with this. Each of us sees him in a personal and unique way. But Christians are agreed that he is more than a prophet or

The Holy Land

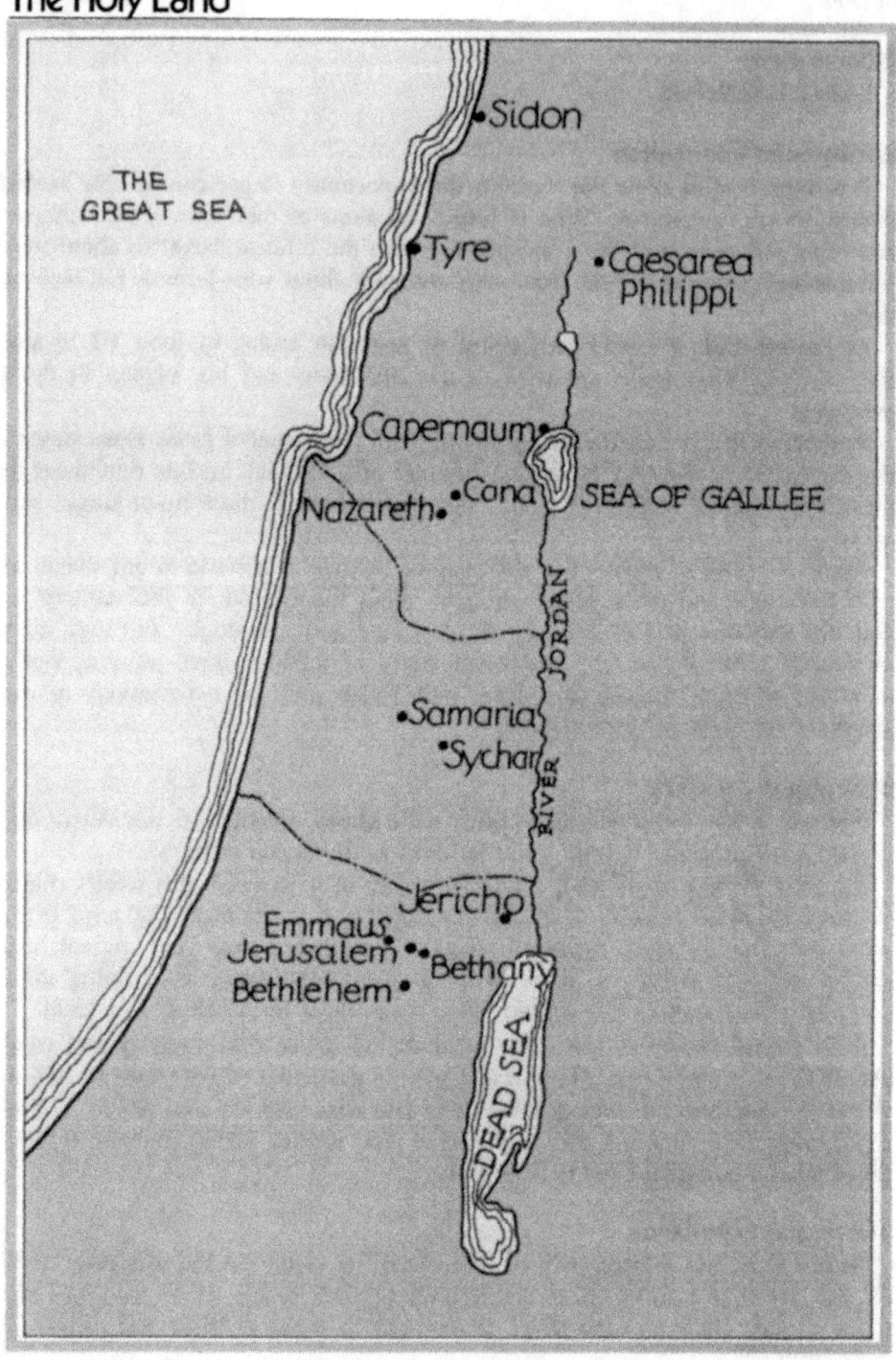

teacher—he is God's chosen one, the Messiah. He is Lord of our lives, our personal Savior.

Does your class remember who Elijah was? Let them review their reading book or notebook to see what they can find about him. Remember the Old Testament stories about his miracles and his mysterious departure in a whirlwind? Can they remember Malachi's prediction that he would return before the end of the world? You may want to reread 1 Kings 17. Whether your students can remember or not, point out that the Jews remembered. Many of them felt that Jesus must be Elijah returning. After all, he performed miracles like Elijah. Even John the Baptist wondered about this.

Prophecy fulfilled. Review the story in Luke 7:11-23 in which John sends messengers to ask Jesus who he is. Jesus answers by saying that what was promised is now happening. Note these promises in Isa. 29:18-19; 35:5-6; and 61:1. It was his way of telling John that his works speak for him.

Have your students take turns reading these passages aloud: Luke 9:7-9; 8:22-25; 8:26-39; 8:40-42; 8:49-56; and 9:10-17. Point out what Jesus was involved in doing. Notice that the people who followed Jesus were beginning to hope and believe he really was the one God had promised. But Herod and his group were becoming convinced that Jesus was a threat to their power and should be eliminated.

Luke tells the story of all these things Jesus did and also the questions people raised about him. Then he retells two stories and some words of Jesus that help put the whole thing together.

Have the story of Peter's confession in Luke 9:18-22 read aloud. Peter spoke for those who had been closest to Jesus, but Jesus asks them to keep who he is a secret. Why does he do this? Because his was not going to be the way of glory as most people were expecting. Both he and his followers would suffer.

Event on the mountain. Then look at the second story about the wonderful vision that Peter, James, and John had on the mountain as told in Luke 9:28-36. Two great men of the Old Testament appear with Jesus before the three disciples: Moses the great law giver, and Elijah the great prophet.

Point out that the Greek word Luke uses for *death* can also be translated *exodus*. Moses and Elijah surely knew what that was—it was God's way to save his people. Here is the story of preparation for Jesus' death—or exodus—as God's way of saving his people.

Why do your students think that the disciples kept silent after this tremendous event? Until Jesus died and rose again, would it have been clear who Jesus really was? The whole mission had not been accomplished, so the secret was kept.

Using the question on the board, "Who do you say that I am?" ask your students to contribute their ideas. Can they remember some of the names we have already heard? *(Messiah, anointed one, David's Son, King of kings, Elijah, Moses, Son of God, Savior, teacher, prophet, Lord, Christ).*

Discuss these words. Point out that some come from Old Testament promises, others tell of the role he was to have for God's people, and some tell how we feel about him or about our relationship to him. Some are titles and others are deeply personal references.

Creative work. We have talked at length about who Jesus was and how people described him so that his followers would know that he was the Son of God. But what does Jesus mean for our lives? Suggest that your class consider some creative way of expressing who Jesus is. They can write songs or poems or use tempera paint to depict their feelings and impressions of the biblical picture of Jesus.

Encourage them to look in their notebooks at their parents' comments about Martin Luther King. What things did the parents say that were factual? Did the story vary from person to person? Did they tell how they felt? How does this assignment relate to people's impressions of Jesus? Ask them to make a personal inventory of how they look at Jesus and what is important about him for their lives. Then encourage them to express themselves in writing or painting. Give enough time to think about the project, checking with each student individually as the work begins; then give supportive suggestions as they go along.

It is important for you to be accepting and free. Encourage them to express their own ideas and feelings. Be positive about ideas and colors that depart from the usual.

Plan to display the writings and paintings if your students feel comfortable with this. Perhaps they can write a brief explanation to go along with their work.

Closing prayer

This session has covered some important theological material and also permitted time for individual creative work. Ask each student to pray a sentence prayer of thanksgiving to God for showing his love for us in Jesus.

Home assignment

Ask the students to read Chapter 24 in the reading book and the assigned biblical material.

Chosen to Serve

Objective
The purpose of this lesson is to point out that Jesus prepared his disciples to carry on the important work of his kingdom, and that we are called to carry on his ministry in three ways: 1) by announcing peace and the coming of the kingdom; 2) by worshiping and praying together; and 3) by taking care of those in need of help.

Biblical basis
Luke 9:51—10:24; 10:38—11:23; 18:1—19:27

Background information
The texts from Luke for this chapter are the story of Jesus and his disciples making their way to Jerusalem. Along the way things happened which provided the disciples with ideas about what Jesus wanted them to do when he was gone. As followers of Christ, we can also learn from these ideas.

You might want to do a bit of research about the ancient use of heralds and messengers. Be prepared with a brief description of the kind of role they have played at various times as announcers and preparers of the way. John the Baptist is a good example of an announcer or preparer of the way.

Preparation for class
There are three tasks for followers of Jesus that will be studied in this week's lesson. As you organize the class material, plan to take a look at the biblical stories which point up each of these tasks. Then relate the three to our role as Christians today by describing ways in which we have these same tasks.

Invite members of the church council or other organizational leaders to explain their task in the church. For example, a deacon (the messenger or servant of those in need) could be invited to describe visits to hospital patients, shut-ins, or prospective members. A panel of various church workers would give the class some idea of what we are to be about as Christians. If it is not possible to have anyone visit, have class members interview several church workers about their tasks and how they perform them. Interviews could be taped and brought to class for listening, or oral reports by students could be made at the next class.

Bring posterboard, felt-tip markers, crayons, and other materials and, if there is time, have the class make triptychs describing "What we are to be about." Each panel of the triptych can represent one of the three roles. Plan to display the triptychs where the congregation can share in this experience.

The lesson experience
Before the class arrives, write across the chalkboard the phrase, "What we are to be about." As your students come to class, talk with them about the lesson, explaining that we will follow Jesus as he made his way from Galilee to Jerusalem, preparing his followers for what was about to happen. He had important work in mind for them and wanted to give them some directions about what they were to be doing after he was gone. If they were to carry on his ministry, they had to know what their task was!

Give your students time to review the chapter and the biblical assignment. Then introduce any people you have invited to class, telling who they are and why you have invited them. Have them read along with the class about the preparation and instruction Jesus gave as he worked with that first group of followers. Provide materials for guests if you can, or ask students to share their materials with them. This will give them a chance to find out what the students have read as a basis for their visit and to get acquainted with your class.

If you are interviewing people during this class hour rather than having a panel of guests, do the chapter and Bible material first, then make sure the assignments are clear. Discuss what the students will be doing before they leave for the interviews. Make sure they have specific questions in mind about the task of Christians. If recorders are available, be certain the students know how to operate them. If oral reports are planned, be clear about what the class will expect to hear.

The work of followers. Can the class recall from the chapter what three things Jesus told his disciples to do? List them on the board and review them one at a time:

1. Announce the kingdom
2. Pray and worship together
3. Take care of those who need help and be alert for the return of the king

1. Jesus sent his disciples ahead of him to announce the kingdom. Luke 9:51-56 describes how the Samaritans didn't want to recognize Jesus as he came, "because his face was set toward Jerusalem." How did Jesus react when the disciples wanted to destroy these people?

In Luke 10:1-16, Jesus gives instructions again. His messengers are to bring a word of peace, and when they are received, they are to heal the sick and bring assurance that the kingdom has come. When rejected, they are to leave with no violence, but with a warning.

These followers are not to judge or punish others who do not accept the message. In Luke 10:20, Jesus tells his disciples that the joy of this kingdom is not in the defeat of others. We aren't sent out to show off. Our task is to proclaim the kingdom, and our joy is in the fact that we are chosen to be messengers of that kingdom.

2. The disciples were to keep in touch through prayer. Jesus told a number of stories about praying and how it should be done. In Luke 11:1-4, Jesus answers their request, "Lord, teach us how to pray" by teaching them the kingdom prayer or Lord's Prayer that we use today. Praying was crucial. It kept Jesus in touch with what his father wanted him to be doing. Jesus wanted the disciples to have that same kind of contact with the father.

3. Finally, Jesus wanted his disciples to serve people. Determining when the kingdom will finally come is God's business. We show how prepared we are for the return of the king by how well we serve him. Can your students recall the parable Jesus told about this situation? Look at Luke 19:11-27 again. The servants of the nobleman had a job to do. When the return finally came, the servant who never got down to work was the one who lost out.

Jesus has work for his followers to do. We are told to care for people who are in need of help just as he did. All during his journey to Jerusalem, Jesus took time for the sick, the lonely, and the outcasts who needed him. His death was coming, but Jesus continued to bring the kingdom of God to people by word and deed.

Our task today. Just as Jesus prepared the disciples for work in his kingdom, so we are instructed to go about our work in our part of the kingdom. Use the panel of guests to describe how your congregation is busy with the work Jesus gave to his followers. Ask them to speak for a few minutes about their group and the ways in which they try to fulfill their tasks. Help them share personal experiences and specific instances in which they have been able to announce the kingdom, pray and worship, or take care of others. You can moderate the panel, but allow the class to ask questions, too.

Can your students think of ways in which they are taking seriously the kind of tasks Jesus has given? At first they may hesitate, but help them talk about ways in which they can announce the kingdom. Do they tell others about Christ and his church? Do they worship regularly and learn about him here in this class? How about the praying we've done together each week? Caring for others is one of the class goals we set at the beginning of the year. Do they find they get a chance to show others they are Christian by caring for them in school and at home? Have the students write in their notebooks two ways in which they personally have been of service. Remember to thank your guests, or if interviews were conducted, ask the students to write brief notes of thanks.

This might be an excellent time to take a few minutes to pray about our job as followers of Jesus. Ask him to help us see what he wants us to do, and then to give us the strength and joy to do it. You could begin this prayer and ask students to join in as they feel ready.

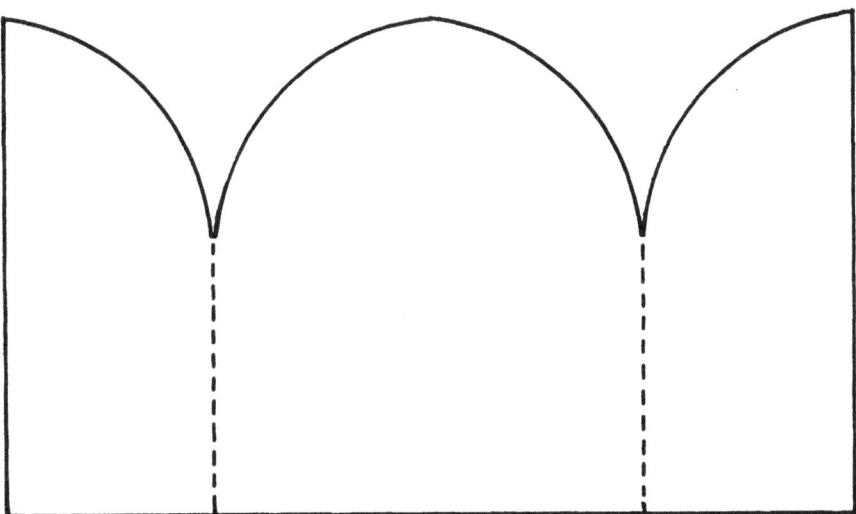

Triptych project. A triptych is a three-panel picture or booklet. The center panel is flanked by two side panels half its size; these fold down over the center panel and cover it. One sheet of poster board can be folded and properly cut. Each one can be decorated as the students wish. They can make their own drawings or use magazine illustrations. Words and phrases describing the three kinds of tasks can be placed on the three panels.

Suggest that your students work together in threes, each doing one panel of a triptych. Let them think of symbols, words, or pictures they might use to describe their part of the task. When the triptychs are closed, they can write on the outside the words "What We Are to Be About." Remember to make the best use of these projects. Perhaps they could be displayed some place where the congregation can enjoy them.

Home assignment

Ask your students to read Chapter 25 in the reading book and the biblical material which is included. If interviews were carried out during the class hour, or are to be done during the week as a home assignment, be sure the students are reminded to bring all their material to class for the next session.

Halfway mark

We are now halfway through the New Testament material and you may want to give a test. If so, announce that there will be a short exam over material covered in lessons 17-24 next week. Ask them to review their chapters and come prepared to spend about 15 minutes on the test.

If you do not wish to use the test during class time, you could have copies made of the questions and send them as a home exam for the students to use during the week and bring completed to class. Allow them to use their books and notebooks to find answers. You may want to write your own exam, based on your own class experiences or use this one.

1. Which of the gospels tell the story of Jesus? *(all of them; Matthew, Mark, Luke, and John).*

2. Name two kinds of books we can find in the New Testament *(gospels; history, like the book of Acts; letters or epistles; apocalypse, the Revelation of John).*

3. Name two types of savior the people of this time were looking for God to send them *(a great king, a prophet, a high priest, a destroyer of the world).*

4. Write one advantage in having four different gospels written by four different men *(Each writes from a different viewpoint; each speaks to different people; some details left out in one are filled in by another; specific needs are met by one or another for each of us).*

5. Why do you think people die? *(because of the broken relationship between God and man, a result of our sin).*

6. How does a Christian face death? *(believing Jesus has overcome it; remembering that the resurrection promises new life).*

7. What great New Testament event declares that God is in charge of the world? *(the resurrection).*

8. How does Jesus become known after his resurrection? *(through word and sacrament; as he prayed with people, talked to them and ate with them).*

9. Why is John the Baptist called the last of the great prophets? *(He prepares or announces the coming of Jesus.)*

10. What question would you ask about a prophet such as Jesus who came claiming to be God's son? *(Does his life-style agree with his talk? Does what he's saying fit into the long story of God and his people? Does he have anything to back up his words?).*

11. What clues do we have that Jesus was a good teacher? *(the crowds that listened, the people who changed because of him).*

12. What name is given to the short stories Jesus told? *(parables).*

13. What might one purpose of the miracles have been? *(to show people he could do what only God can do).*

14. Why did some people think Jesus might be Elijah? *(He performed similar miracles; it was predicted he would return at the end of the world).*

15. Who does Peter say that Jesus is when Jesus asks him? *(the Christ of God).*

16. Name two things Jesus expects us as his disciples to be about *(announcing the kingdom, praying and worshiping, taking care of those in need).*

17. Why should we continue to pray and worship together? *(It keeps us in touch with God and one another; we learn what God wants us to do.)*

18. How do we know when the final coming of the kingdom will be? *(It's not our business—we have been given important work to do and shouldn't waste time trying to figure out when it will come; we know it will come in God's good time).*

19. Where was Jesus heading during the time we have just studied? *(on his way to Jerusalem).*

20. Why did Jesus teach his disciples the Lord's Prayer? *(They asked him to help them pray; he wanted them to learn to pray).*

Hail to the Chief

Objective
The purpose of this lesson is to sharpen the issue of who Jesus is. It should help members of the class think through their relationship with Jesus.

Biblical basis
Luke 19:28—20:40

Background information
In his triumphal entry Jesus made it plain that he was the king. He entered Jerusalem with fanfare and with many followers, fulfilling prophecy. At the same time we find opposition to him increasing. There were those who wanted to destroy him. Again and again they attempted to trap Jesus.

The story of the death of Jesus came at the beginning of this New Testament study. It might be good to review that chapter in preparation for this class. You may want to use a small portion of class time to review the significant events of Chapter 18. The advantage of having already had that lesson is that you can now concentrate on the action, knowing the outcome. It's a little like seeing a play or movie after you've read the book—you know the ending and can see more clearly how it came about. Help your class to look closely at the people and events that led up to Jesus' death and resurrection. Emphasize the fact that people still have trouble accepting Jesus as king, and they try to get rid of him in one way or another.

Preparation for class
The rock opera *Jesus Christ Superstar* has an excellent section of music and dialog about the entry into Jerusalem and the beginnings of the plot against Jesus by the religious leaders. Try to use the section, "This Jesus Must Die" through "Hosanna" and "Poor Jerusalem." Play the music and listen to the words, or better yet, have copies of the libretto available for the class to follow as they listen. Then discuss what you have heard.

This might be another good time to use a taped interview to help your students better understand some of the biblical people involved in the Palm Sunday account. Bring a tape recorder if you have one. Otherwise, simply assign students to play the roles of characters involved. Ask them to write a letter, a report, or a description of Jesus from that person's point of view. This would help the class understand how people saw Jesus in different ways and responded according to their own viewpoints.

Informal drama could be used instead of the tapes. Assign roles to your students and ask them to act out the biblical material. Make sure they use their Bibles to get into what actually happened. Then encourage them to write their own parts, filling in personalities, reactions, and dialog. The class could talk through the scenes, discussing what characters were likely to say and do and helping classmates develop their roles.

An optional activity could be a real entry into Jerusalem staged by your class for Sunday services or for another class. Spend your time planning a parade for Jesus. Update the story to modern times. Make placards and banners declaring Jesus to be the king for whom we've waited (or instead of king you could use the words "leader" or "president." Perhaps the people would shout, "Jesus for president!" Religious leaders would be pastors, deacons, and council members who are threatened by this man Jesus. The planning and discussion involved in the parade is an opportunity to discuss people's reactions to Jesus.

The lesson experience
If you plan to give an exam, do it first. This enables the class to be more at ease for the rest of the class. If you haven't prepared the class, but wish to use

the test as a quiz allowing them to use their books, then introduce it as a review test. Be sure to allow time to discuss the answers either in this class or the next session.

Then open with a "popcorn" prayer, suggesting that each person think about what we have learned in these lessons concerning Jesus' ministry. Give them a few minutes to think, then begin the prayer yourself, allowing class members to join in with their petitions at any time. A popcorn prayer is spontaneous, so they shouldn't worry about more than one person thinking of things to say at the same time. The leader can encourage "popping" by suggesting such things as, "We're grateful, Jesus, that you taught us about . . . how much you care for us . . . that we are your children . . ." Your students can add their own ideas from this basic starter. Silences are all right, too. You can close the prayer with a sentence about the kind of decision we must make about Jesus, and ask God to help us make him the master of our lives.

Into the chapter. Give the class a few minutes to review Chapter 25. While they are doing this, put up any art work you have about the entry into Jerusalem. If you are going to use a recording, set up the player and have it ready to go.

Then talk about the entry into Jerusalem. What things can the students remember about it? Of what significance were the colt, the palm branches, and the garments thrown on the ground? How would this have happened today? Would there be ticker tape, confetti, banners, and signs? Who would be the modern-day hero? Who would be the enemies? Newspaper clippings or magazine pictures of the president touring or a leader surrounded by followers or protesters would be helpful in this discussion.

It is apparent that many believed Jesus to be the promised one for whom they had waited so long. It's also clear from the Luke account that others felt he was a dangerous leader, and definitely not what they wanted for a king. They were unable and unwilling to accept him and began to plot his end.

Much of the opposition to Jesus came from religious leaders who lived by the law and began to trust it more than they did God. Are there people who do this today? Try to think of examples of how we may trust our keeping of the law more than we trust God's promise.

Ask the question, "Who killed Jesus?" List possible answers on the board—the Romans, Pilate, the Jews. Ask if they sometimes make the kind of decisions and mistakes which resulted in Jesus' death. Each of us has to bear some responsibility here. Be sure to talk about the believers, too. There were many, including Jesus' followers, who felt that he was the king. They cheered him.

This would be the time to play parts of *Jesus Christ Superstar*, especially the section, "This Jesus Must Die." The dialog describes the mixed feelings of people surrounding Jesus. Let the students listen and comment. Do they feel it's possible to have been around Jesus and to react in this way? Who were these people, and who would these people be today if Jesus had come in our time?

Any art work you've gathered could be discussed at this point. What expressions do they see on the faces of the people? What's exciting about the kind of crowd and display put on for Jesus on that Sunday? What's frightening about such a crowd? Where might one's enemies be in this case? If this happened today, could you tell the followers from the enemies? Do they know of any experiences where leaders of today have had enemies mixed in with believers and loyal followers? Jesus knew the risks, but he chose to bring the kingdom in this way.

Once the class is clear as to what the chapter says and what it means in terms of Jesus' death, you can move to some creative kinds of activities. Choose one or more of these optional activities, depending on how much time you have.

If you choose to do a taped interview, assign students the roles of Jesus, Caiaphas, disciples, priests, Roman soldiers, the man who owned the colt, etc. Using your Bibles, ask them to write an interview in their own words about their experiences with Jesus during these events. How did they feel about him, about the crowds around him, about what was going to happen? Did they think he would destroy the world, become the king, die, or what? Jesus might say how he felt, what he knew was coming, what he hoped for, what he worried about. Tape all the parts one at a time. You could be the interviewer, or you could assign that part. Play it back for the class to review and enjoy.

If you choose to do an informal drama, provide some simple props. Work as a class to prepare the parts in a simple drama with impromptu dialog that your class creates as they discuss the events. Rehearse it as it develops, and if it comes off well, perhaps your class could share it with another group or class.

A parade for Jesus would give your students an opportunity to present Jesus to others and to acknowledge him as leader. They could make signs and banners, and plan a parade in a worship service or in another class. How do they want to impress people? What do they want to say? What reactions can they expect? To follow up, you might analyze what people's responses were and why.

Reflection time. As the class comes to a close, give your students a few minutes to think about this lesson. Ask them each to write a short paragraph in their notebooks under the heading, "Who Is Jesus?" The words should reflect their classroom experiences. How does each feel about Jesus and his ministry, about those who followed him, and about those who plotted his death? But most of all, about Jesus. What does it mean to be a follower of Jesus?

This reflective time may very well set a mood for a fellowship prayer. If you sense that this would be a good closing, gather the class into a circle and suggest they join hands as a symbol of fellowship and sharing as Jesus' followers. Ask for a moment of silent prayer, giving an opportunity to reflect and search within about our relationship to Jesus. Close the prayer when a few minutes have passed.

Home assignment

Ask the students to read Chapter 26 for next week, including the assigned biblical material.

It's a New Day

Objective

The purpose of this lesson is to present the Pentecost story. Pentecost is the birthday of the church when the disciples, empowered by the Holy Spirit, witnessed in Jerusalem. We are promised the same Spirit, and called to be witnesses. God uses people like us to tell his story!

Biblical basis

Acts 1:1—2:24, 37-42

Background information

Pentecost is still celebrated as a festival during our church year. Spend some time researching the colors, symbols, and suggested activities for this day; then incorporate them into your classroom experience if it fits your group. The class might work together on making a large Pentecost banner. Encourage them to cooperate, with each student contributing to the project.

Acts 1:7-8 could be dealt with in some depth. The references to Jerusalem (right where you are), then Judea (your neighbors and those around you), then Samaria (people considered outsiders), and to the end of the earth (people everywhere who need to hear God's story), carries many implications. The call to witness to the world is an important concept for Christians. It challenges us to move beyond the realm of our own selfish interests—to reach out with the good news.

Preparation for class

You will have to decide how much emphasis you wish to place on the idea of speaking in tongues in regard to the Pentecost experience and the gift of the Holy Spirit. Perhaps some of your students will be interested enough to want to research this and present a report to the class in the next session. This would allow you more time to complete the lesson and still give an opportunity to investigate the topic. If you have a church library, one or two students could do some research there. If not, they might consult with the pastor for his insights and any resources he could suggest.

Bring materials to class for banner making if this is the sort of thing your group enjoys doing. Look for information on the church year and its festivals, particularly material on Pentecost. If your church has an altar guild, perhaps it could be of some help. Provide felt, burlap, or cotton, as well as fabric scraps, yarn, trim, and anything else suitable to creative work.

Print Acts 1:7-8 on a large piece of poster board and place it where everyone can see it. During the class use the verse in as many ways as you can, repeating it whenever it comes up. Ask the class to read it together in the Bible at least once; plan to try some word games using this verse; and locate Jerusalem, Judea, and Samaria on the Holy Land map on page 109 of the student book. By the end of the class, most of the students will have the verse memorized.

If you wish to use the Scramble Graph, make copies in advance so that each student has a copy to look for the words. You may photocopy the puzzle from page 95 of this guide. As this activity is completed, these words can be written on the board and discussed.

The lesson experience

Be sure that Acts 1:7-8 is up and visible as your students arrive. Ask them to repeat this verse with you as you open the session. How do they interpret the verse? What does Chapter 26 in the reading book say about it? If the same instructions were given today, what places might be substituted for Jerusalem, Judea, and Samaria? Discuss the idea of witnessing to the world. How does it affect us as Jesus' disciples today?

Scramble Graph

```
E P M O T J E S U S P H S U W
A O C Y O U P O N H E A A O H
R W O R L D C T S A N S M Y I
T E M W S E P E F L T W A K C
H R E V N A L N I L E A R T H
T I M E S P C D X M C E I D B
L X B Y I T H E E N O T A W S
B U T C F A L L D S S I N H E
O F S A N D A T A C T S D E A
W I T N E S S E S I A N D N S
D R Y O U K R R S P I R I T O
X E E R L O E L U H I S A C N
T H E L F H E W T H E R X N S
T J A U T H O R I T Y Y I N D
F H H A S N R K L M H H O L Y
S X F P K R E C E I V E J U P
```

The entire quotation of Jesus' words in Acts 1:7-8 is included in this Scramble Graph. Find the words in the passage by reading forward, backward, up, down, or diagonally up or down.

Draw a circle around each word in the puzzle when you find it. Words sometimes cross or overlap and letters may be used more than once.

In addition to Jesus' words you will also find other words related to the Pentecost story. They are listed below.

- WORLD
- FIRE
- PENTECOST
- DISCIPLES
- JESUS
- UP
- ACTS

Rebus   Hint: see Acts 1:8

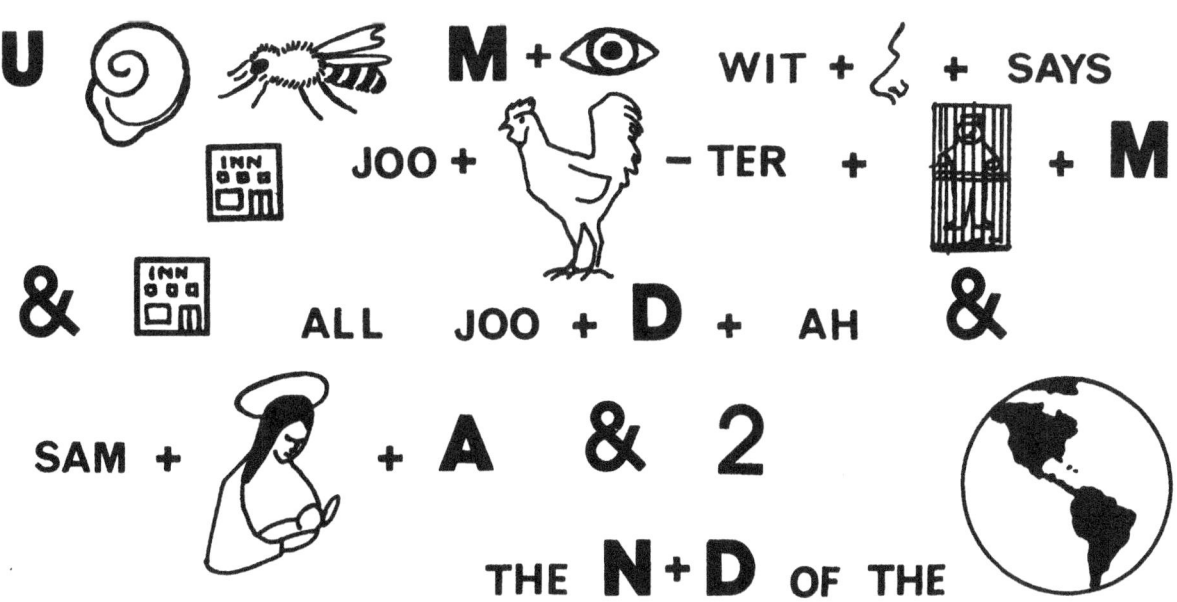

© 1976 Augsburg Publishing House

Give your class a few minutes to write a sentence prayer in their notebooks about this verse. How does it describe our task as Christians? Then ask several students to lead the class in an opening prayer, using the sentences they have written.

Getting into the chapter. Allow the class a few minutes to review Chapter 26 and the biblical material. Then begin by discussing the title of the book of Acts. Why was it so named? Emphasize that it was written to tell what the followers of Jesus did after his ascension.

What events are told about in Acts? As you discuss this, have your students list the events in their notebooks. The events would include such things as the Pentecost story, miracles, shipwrecks, jailbreaks arranged by angels, magicians, death for cheaters. What do they think the book is really about? What has it taught them?

Who are some of the people involved in the events in Acts? Here the class can see again that we're reading about people, good and bad, powerful and weak. God uses people to tell his story, bring his kingdom, and heal his sick. Do your students know any people like this today? If so, help them to begin talking about how God uses people, what kind of people he uses, and the fact that his Spirit works through imperfect human beings. Peter and Paul did important work, but they were not perfect people. God chooses to use people like us; people who make mistakes.

Why is Pentecost called the birthday of the Christian church? Look at Acts 2 again as a class. How do your students explain what is found there? Let them express their ideas. Give them the opportunity to ask questions. Don't be too quick with your answers. Then review the paragraphs in Chapter 26 which remind us that it isn't easy to explain exactly what happened or how. One thing is certain: the Holy Spirit worked a great miracle, with the result that witnesses went out to "turn the world upside down" for Jesus Christ.

Pentecost reminds us that the Holy Spirit did not desert the followers of Jesus. The same Spirit is with us today. Can your students think of symbols for the Holy Spirit: fire, tongues of flame, the dove? Can they remember how the dove descended during Jesus' baptism? Can they think of other stories of the people of God where the symbol of fire represented the presence of God—such as the pillar of fire which led the Israelites or the story of Moses and the burning bush?

What do your students think is the most important part of the Pentecost story? The tongues of fire? The people speaking in many tongues? Notice that only a few verses are given to all the spectacular events, but many verses to Peter's sermon. And notice how much Peter uses the Scriptures and how Jesus is at the center of his message. It's the same story we've been involved with all year. God loves us and he never gives up!

Bring out any material you've been able to gather about Pentecost. Note that it occurs in the church year 10 days after the festival of the Ascension. Red is the color for Pentecost. The altar, lectern, pulpit, and pastor's stole are all red for Pentecost. Why is this an appropriate color? Show the class the pastor's stole and the altar hangings used for Pentecost. Note the color and the symbols on these.

If you intend to have them make banners, this would be the time. Discuss an appropriate design and any wording they might want to put on the banner. What colors will they use? First, work out the design on paper, then divide the class into smaller groups to cut out lettering, paste or sew symbols, draw, and any other tasks that need to be done. The finished product should be one large banner, appropriate for hanging in your church, chapel, or church school area. If there isn't time to finish the banner in class, maybe several students would volunteer to finish it during the week.

Word games. The Scramble Graph and memory work is a project which can be optional. If your group works on a banner and takes the time to do it well, you may have to leave the work on the memory verse until another week as a review or use it as a take-home project.

The Scramble Graph can be fun for people who enjoy working puzzles and word games. Hand out copies of it and ask your students to read the printed directions. They should keep their Bibles open to Acts 1:7-8 as they work so that the verse is in front of them as they search for it on the graph.

It may be easier for them if they just look for any words contained in the verse. Suggest they write the verse in their notebook in large print. As they find a word on the Scramble Graph, they could circle it there and then in their notebook. This way they will be able to keep track of how many words they have found.

A game can be made of the Scramble Graph by setting a time limit. The winner is the person who finds the most words in the allotted time. Teams could be chosen and the group could work on the project together.

An important part of the puzzle work is the discussion of the words of the verse and the supplementary words which are added. The extra words describe things or people important to the story. Write the words on the board and talk about their significance to the verse and to the story. By the time this activity is completed, every student should have memorized the verse.

Another way of zeroing in on the verse to be memorized is to make a rebus. A rebus is a series of symbols and letters combined to bring a message. Note the rebus here in the teacher's guide. Before class, copy it on a large piece of poster board so your students can study it. Then let them try to make up a rebus of their own. They may surprise you with the ideas they have for symbols.

Closing prayer

Ask the students to repeat with you Acts 1:7-8. Then suggest that two or three lead the class in prayer, remembering the lesson we have had concerning the work of the Holy Spirit and our call to witness for Jesus.

Home assignment

Ask the students to read Chapter 27 and the biblical material involved in that chapter before coming to class next week.

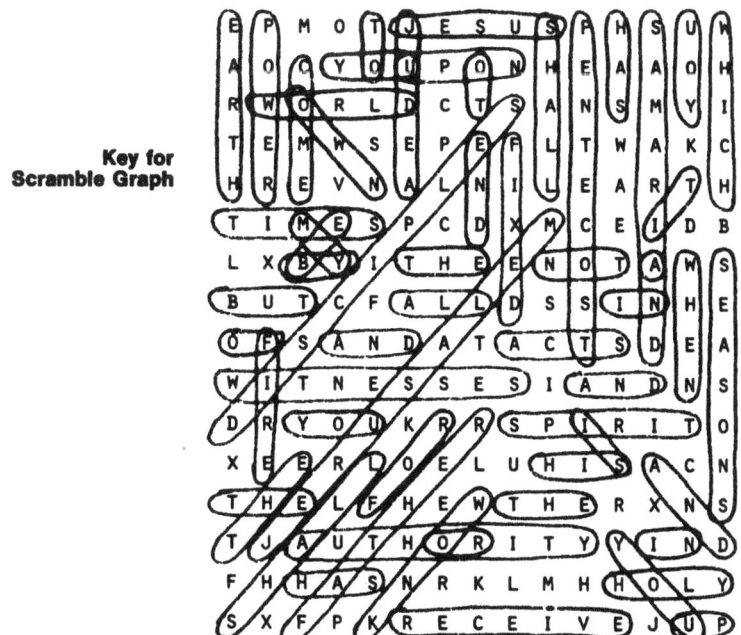

Key for Scramble Graph

Dangerous Business

Objective

The purpose of this lesson is to present examples of Christian witnessing in the early church. Such witnessing was often dangerous business. Christians were persecuted and sometimes killed. And we are called to be witnesses.

Biblical basis

Acts 5:12—8:3

Background information

The story of Stephen and his martyrdom may be familiar to your students. The dangers and difficulties encountered by followers of Christ in the early church are probably less familiar. In this session we shall spend time two ways:

1. There will be Bible study in which we actually read and discuss the accounts of persecution in the book of Acts. Rather than suppressing the good news, we will note that persecution caused it to spread.

2. There will be experiential opportunities for personal witness. A field trip is probably the best way to do this. It could be done during your class time, or on a day shortly before or after you study this chapter.

The Reformation work of Martin Luther could be studied during this session. If you decide to pursue this project, do some research into Luther's life and work. Or invite your pastor to make a brief presentation about Luther's witness and the resulting persecutions. Excerpts from a film about Martin Luther might also be helpful in pointing out the opposition he met from the organized church.

Preparation for class

In preparation for this class, first decide which projects you want to do. If you want to use something about Martin Luther, you will need to prepare carefully and allot the necessary class time. Plan discussion questions which focus on the witness of Luther. The film could be used for family night, combining the ideas of witnessing and sharing the good news with families and friends. Invite the families of your class to view the film and to join the discussion after it is shown.

If you choose to use the field trip, carefully plan and publicize it. Such a trip would be a good opportunity for your class to get involved in witnessing and maybe also discover some of the feelings related to this week's chapter. Consider these possibilities:

1. Visit some of the shut-ins in your community, sharing with them the good news that God loves us and is with us always. Plan a brief devotion the students can present in teams of three or four. It might be helpful to have copies of the devotion available for all members of your teams.

2. Plan a shopper's treat for one of the downtown areas in your community. Prepare cookies or bars for giving away along with the spoken message, "God loves you and so do I." Observe people's reactions as the offer and witness is made to them.

3. Visit a nursing home in your area and present a brief program of singing, prayer, Bible reading, and personal witness about God's love for his people.

Proper preparation for such trips is important, as is the opportunity to evaluate the experience after it is over. Each student should be encouraged to write an evaluation of where the class went, what was done, how people responded, how the students felt about it, and what was learned from the experience. The class should have an opportunity to share their evaluations. Often what is missed by one student will be picked up by someone else. You need to be a resource person. Be on hand to help when words fail a student or to help them get started. Be sure to allow time to organize the groups and to get them to and from the destination.

The lesson experience

Give your students a few minutes to review the chapter and biblical material as they arrive. Again use the poster board with the quotation from Acts 1:7-8. Place it where everyone can see it. Can they remember the main themes of the last session on the Pentecost experience?

Our concern in this session is with people who took Jesus' orders seriously. Witnessing to the truth was not always easy, but in the midst of persecution and difficulty and sometimes even death, they found that God was present with them.

Write the word *witness* on the blackboard. What does the word mean? List their synonyms for the word and anything else they can tell you about its origin. Our chapter tells us that the Greek word for witness was *martyr*. The word came to mean "someone who dies for what he or she believes" simply because so many Christian witnesses were persecuted or killed.

Who became martyrs? Students will probably name Stephen, Peter, and perhaps some of the other disciples and early church leaders. Whom do they consider to be martyrs today? Does anyone know who Bonhoeffer was? How about Martin Luther King? Was he a martyr? Help them list a few people they feel were martyrs because of their witness to the truth. Discuss what it means to be a witness.

A witness is someone with a message. The task of the witness is to deliver the message. In this case the message is the story of God and his love for his people. It's the story of Jesus, his ministry and his sacrifice for us.

Look at Acts 5 and note the accounts of the amazing power God gave his witnesses, but also the persecution they often had to endure. Discuss these things with your class. What enabled them to witness as they did and to endure the persecution? How do your students account for this? What is the promise found in the memory verse from the last lesson? Does this promise have anything to do with us?

In studying Stephen, be aware of the words *Hebrew* and *Hellenist*. Write them on the board and ask your students to write them in their notebooks. The Hebrews were probably Jewish Christians who had always lived in or around Jerusalem, and the Hellenists were probably Jewish Christians who came from cities and countries where Greek was spoken. The Hellenists were accused of not respecting Moses, God, the temple, or the law, and of trying to change the religious customs of the people. Acts 6 describes how Stephen was accused of all these things.

Discuss the controversy between the two groups. How did the apostles settle this argument? Stephen emerged as one of the seven chosen to end the bickering, and he turns out to be a powerful witness. His death is an example of what hatred can do. Those who stirred up the people against him were angry and afraid of his witness.

Acts 7 should be carefully studied. It is Stephen's defense of himself, and also an excellent review of some of the outstanding people in the Old Testament. Read it together. Point out how the story reveals the greatness of God and his love for his people. But Stephen also very bluntly revealed the unfaithfulness of God's people, and pointed out how they killed Jesus, the very one the prophets had announced. Stephen enraged the Jews and they killed him, with the result that a great persecution began and the apostles were scattered throughout Judea and Samaria (remember Acts 1:7-8). Persecution, terrible as it was, resulted in the spread of the gospel. Jesus' order to be his witnesses was being fulfilled.

Looking at our own witness. Whom would your students add to their list of witnesses to the gospel today? Would they include their pastor, their family, their teachers at church school, themselves?

What kind of witness are we to give? What do your students think it means to witness? Does it mean we are to stand on a street corner, be preachers, give our lives as missionaries, or what?

Discuss how witnessing can be a part of our everyday experiences. Most of us will never be called on to give our life for our faith. But we are called on to tell others about God's love when the opportunity comes. Can the class think of situations in which they have had a chance to witness? Have they done so? Perhaps you can share some incidents from your own life: a time when someone else's witness meant a great deal; or a time when you missed an opportunity to witness; or a time when there were amazing results from what appeared to be a simple act of witnessing on your part.

Discuss the idea of the power of God's Spirit. What makes it hard or easy to witness? How do we know when there is an appropriate time to talk about our faith? Help the class share their concerns about sounding ridiculous and imposing on others' freedom. Share the promise that God's Spirit will be with us. Can we trust him to use us at the right moment? Do we depend too much on our own resources, or do we believe that what Jesus promised the disciples is his promise to us as well?

This is the time to ready your group for the field trip if it is planned for a date before your next class. Or if the film and family night are coming up, remind your class members of the schedule and plans.

Closing prayer

How about a "popcorn" prayer asking God to help us to tell his story whenever the appropriate time comes and thanking him for the many witnesses he has provided to carry his story through the ages to us.

Home assignment

Ask your students to read Chapter 28 for next week. If you have plans for a field trip later or the film will be shown at a different time, be sure you remind them of the necessary details—transportation, publicity, invitations, equipment, cookies to be given away, and the proper thank-yous to those involved in the project.

Objective

The purpose of this lesson is to examine the deep and important change that took place in the life of Paul, his conversion experience. God, who calls each of us to be his witnesses, can work such changes in our lives, too.

Biblical basis

Acts 9:1-31; 15:1-29

Background information

Again in this session, we meet the theme of the power of God's Holy Spirit to change people. Paul was changed from a persecuter to a witness. There were dramatic changes in the early church when it began to accept Gentiles. And God has changed our lives, too, by the power of his Word and sacraments.

Remember that Paul, before his conversion, was a God-fearing Jew. He had been steeped in the law of Moses and knew as well as anyone the rules Jews were to follow. The significance of the change in his life was that now the focus of his attention was turned from the law and its fulfillment, to Jesus and the acceptance of God's forgiveness and love through him.

In the background of the next three chapters is the problem of the conflict between the early Christians and Jewish traditions, particularly about the law. Do some research into Jewish traditions and practices. If there is a synagogue in your community, perhaps your class could visit it, meet the rabbi, and learn something about the rituals of circumcision, Scripture reading, food laws, festivals, etc. This visit could be made any time during the next three sessions, though it would be helpful to make it now as a background to these lessons. It could help your class to better understand the struggle Paul had with some of the early congregations.

Preparation for class

Plan a visit to the synagogue if you can. If there is none nearby, perhaps a Jewish friend could explain the rituals of the Jewish religion. Be sure to give plenty of time for this field trip. Make your arrangements with the rabbi in advance. Let him know you want your class to develop an appreciation of the Jewish tradition.

The map of the early Christian world will be helpful for this lesson. Also refer the class to the map of Paul's missionary journeys, found inside the back cover of the student book. Bring back the poster board with the quotation from Acts 1:7-8. It can be the center of a brief review and a reminder that as disciples, we are given orders from Jesus to bring his message to all the world.

One idea for depicting change might be to gather for the bulletin board a number of pictures showing change. Examples could come from the seasons, the caterpillar and butterfly, the baby that becomes an adult, the seed and flower, etc. You could ask your students to bring pictures of such changes, or draw symbols or pictures during the next few weeks and add them to the board.

The lesson experience

As the class arrives, let them help you display the pictures and the quotation on the bulletin board. If you are visiting the synagogue during this class session, begin by thinking of questions to ask, or by sharing questions you have already prepared.

After your return, be sure to take time to evaluate the experience. Ask the students what impressed them most, what questions they have about what was said, and how they feel about what happened. Discuss the things we share in common with the Jewish people, as well as our differences. Help them to ap-

Friend or Foe?

preciate the visit and also to discuss the problem that Paul had as a changed person in beginning to work with the early Christians.

Give the students a few minutes to look over the chapter and the biblical material for this week. While they are doing this, make sure you have your "change" pictures up, and get out your map and the quotation if they are not already in place.

Begin with a question such as, "Do you believe a person can really be changed?" What kinds of things change people? Are there special times in our lives that we might point to as turning points or changes that are really significant? Do we know anyone who seems completely different, for better or worse, from the way he or she used to be? Maybe your class will begin to see the problem Ananias had in Acts 9:10-19. He couldn't believe his ears. God was asking him to go to Saul, one of the great persecutors of Christians, and help him. How would your students feel if this vision had come to them?

Saul was a great defender of the law of Moses who became one of the most effective servants the church would ever know. God can work great changes. He had plans for Saul, and Saul's background in Scripture and Jewish life were not wasted. Note what happened when Saul's conversion occurred. His old friends didn't approve, and some of them tried to kill him. His former enemies, the Christians, ended up protecting him.

Remember that the first Christians were Jewish. They went to the temple for special events, worshipped in the synagogue, and celebrated the festivals and rituals of their Jewish fathers before them. They expected Gentile Christians to observe Jewish rituals and life-style. This was the issue that caused the first church convention.

Review what our chapter has to say about the Jerusalem Council. The issue was an important one. The church made it clear that Gentile believers did not have to become Jewish in order to become Christians. After the Jerusalem Council the church would never be the same again. Give your students a few minutes to write a short paragraph in their notebooks about the council and the main issues discussed there.

Have your class think about the changes that were made in Paul's life because God called him to work for his kingdom—he had a new name and a new life. They should also think about what God calls them to do and how it might change their lives. Suggest spending a few minutes in silence and then lead the group in prayer, thanking God for his Spirit and the great work he can do with us when we are willing to change. Ask for his presence with us during the coming week.

Then discuss change with your class. Young people feel they are very open to change. This is true in some areas. They seem to adjust well to schedule changes, new books, and fads. But what about important changes? Has any member of the class ever moved? Has anyone ever had a new parent or family? How did they adjust to the change?

The central idea here is that God can work change in us even when we feel it is impossible. He can bring good from things that seem difficult. He can use our mistakes and our bad times to change other people.

We often hear parents and others talk about the "good old days." How do the students react to that phrase? What days do they feel are the good ones?

Can the class think of ways in which being a Christian has changed their lifestyle? Can they give specific instances of how God changed their mind or their behavior toward someone else? The story of Paul is another reminder that God uses all kinds of people for his purposes. Saul, a Jewish legalist, turned out to be one of his most effective witnesses. So there's hope for us. God can change us if we allow him to use us.

If there is time, introduce the map and the places on it which we will be talking about during the next two weeks as we see Paul at work for the kingdom. Do the students recognize any of the cities named? Begin by locating Jerusalem, the holy city of the Jewish people, where the Council met in A.D. 49. From there we know Paul visited many places. Can your students find some of them?

Home assignment

Ask your students to read Chapter 29 and the biblical material contained in it. Have them write in their notebooks a list of all the books of the New Testament and to circle those they think Paul might have written. Next week we shall take a closer look at some of them. And you may want to let the students know that a short quiz will be given during the next session.

29

Hang On to the Gospel

Objective
The purpose of this lesson is to present the gospel as the good news of God's love and forgiveness in Jesus Christ. God has done everything necessary for our salvation in Jesus Christ. Our salvation does not depend upon our good works or keeping of the law. This was the message proclaimed by Paul and it is your privilege to proclaim it to your students.

Biblical basis
Galatians 1-2

Background information
Paul ran into opposition from individuals and congregations who kept insisting that God would only save people who kept all of the Old Testament laws. Paul knew this was contrary to the good news of God's love and forgiveness in Jesus Christ. He boldly stated that those who preached and taught and thought otherwise were deserting the gospel. God's forgiveness in Jesus Christ is a free gift meant for all people, Jews and Gentiles. God's Son has made us free—this was Paul's theme. He and other disciples wrote the New Testament epistles to preserve this great theme.

Preparation for class
Make a poster listing the first 14 New Testament epistles. Write the names large enough so they can be easily seen and so there is room to write additional information about each book: Romans, 1 and 2 Corinthians, Galatians, Ephesians, Philippians, Colossians, 1 and 2 Thessalonians, 1 and 2 Timothy, Titus, Philemon, and Hebrews.

You might want to bring to class several resource books such as Bible dictionaries and commentaries which your students can use if they want to do additional research on any of these epistles. Also remember to make use of the map of the early New Testament world, especially noting Corinth, Galatia, Ephesus, Philippi, Colossae, and Thessalonica so your class can visualize where Paul had been. This map is printed inside the back cover of the student book.

Your bulletin board theme this week can be letters. Bring a stack of old letters for display on the bulletin board. Briefly discuss why they are important to you. Communicate the idea that our New Testament epistles came to us originally as personal notes from one Christian to others. They were saved for the same reason that we save important mail today—to reread and enjoy again and again.

Also plan to review your visit to the synagogue and the things learned about Jewish practices. This review can lay the foundation for the issues Paul was fighting with the Galatians, and the stand he took on Christian freedom. Leave a little time for writing a thank-you note to the hosts at the synagogue. Let your class compose and write it in appreciation. Writing a letter also ties in with our theme of letters or epistles.

The lesson experience
A review might be a good way to introduce the subject matter of this lesson. Give your students a chance to share their impressions of the synagogue visit, especially what was said about Jewish laws. Remember to write the thank-you note. If you did not make such a visit, then simply discuss the main points of last week's lesson.

One way to review would be to give a brief quiz. Once it is completed, correct it in class as a further means of review. Here are some questions you could use:

1. What is someone who is not a Jew called? *(a Gentile)*.

2. When God appeared to Ananias and asked for his help, why was he afraid to visit Saul? *(Saul was known as a persecutor of Christians)*.

3. What was our memory passage found in Acts 1:7-8?

4. What was the nationality of the first Christians and what did they think was necessary in order to be a Christian? *(They were Jews and they thought it was necessary to become Jewish in order to be Christian).*

5. What occasion celebrates the coming of the Holy Spirit? *(Pentecost).*

6. What is the color for this celebration of the church's birthday? *(red).*

7. Who became the first Christian martyr? *(Stephen).*

8. What does the word *martyr* mean? *(a witness who gives up his life for what he believes).*

9. Who were the Hellenists? *(probably Jewish Christians who came from cities and countries where Greek was spoken).*

10. How many books are there in the New Testament? *(27).*

Find out how many students have read the home assignment. Give them all a few minutes to review it again. Then they should open their notebooks to the list they were to make of the New Testament books, circling those that they think were written by Paul.

Have your students turn to their New Testaments. Remind your class that the gospels are placed first not because they were written first, but because they tell the central story on which all the others depend—the story of Jesus our Savior.

Then assign the rest of the New Testament books to individual students who should look them up in their Bibles, trying to discover who might have written each book, when, to whom, and why. They should read only a few verses and then share with the group what they have found. Can they draw any conclusions from reading just a few verses? How many different authors have they come across? How important is Paul as a letter writer? According to our reading book, which epistles are the oldest? Remind your class that these early letters are the oldest books in the New Testament. Some were probably written 10 to 20 years before the gospels were written.

What do the students know about epistles? Let your class share ideas gleaned from the chapter *(They were expensive, had to be carried by messenger, were written on handmade paper or leather).* Why were they written? Do you suppose more letters were written besides the ones appearing in our New Testament? If you were able to find some Bible dictionaries and commentaries in your church library or borrowed them from your pastor, use them now. Have your students work in pairs. Let each pair choose one of the 14 epistles you have on the board. Ask them to find two interesting facts about the epistle in the dictionary or commentary. It is not necessary to investigate all 14 epistles. Spend a short time sharing the information found.

Getting into Galatians. We shall be focusing on the letter to the Galatians, which was written to the people living in the province of Galatia, which was in Asia Minor. Paul wrote the letter because he was upset with the churches.

The contents of the letter to Galatia describe the problem. Paul declared to the Christians of Galatia that God's love and forgiveness was meant for everybody. He was angry with them because they seemed unwilling to accept the decision of the Jerusalem Council. (Do your students remember that convention and what the church decided?) Paul defended himself and made an important declaration of Christian freedom.

Look at the letter to the Galatians. Move from member to member of your class, reading the two Bible chapters assigned in the reading book, Galatians 1–2, to find out what Paul has to say in this letter and what his message is for us today. Paul says we do not have to qualify for God's love by keeping the law.

Paul laid it on the line. He was truly an apostle through "Jesus Christ and God the Father who raised him from the dead." He made it clear that he wasn't taking orders from some human agency—his orders came from God in Christ. Paul felt his call as strongly as any of the Old Testament prophets.

Paul's conversion is something we looked at before. What can the students remember about it? Paul felt his background qualified him and prepared him for what God called him to do. He had an intense love for the law of Moses, but now he saw it in proper perspective. The law was not the basis for salvation, but we keep the law because of God's love which has reached out to us.

This is an important concept. The Galatians are not the only ones who have trouble when they confuse the purpose of the law and try to earn God's love. In what ways do we do this? You will want to help your students talk this through. Paul stresses that God had already accepted him because of Jesus Christ; God had made a new covenant through Christ.

Again review Chapter 7 and take a look at the explanation of the purpose of the law in that chapter. It was given as a gift to us to help us live in the world God created. It was a result of God's love, and not meant to help us qualify for that love.

How about us? Do we get caught in the same trap as the Galatians? Can we believe the gospel or not? Paul makes it clear that anybody trying to play the "qualifying" game is just plain wrong—it never works.

How would your students answer if someone asked them, "How do you get God to love you?" or "What should you do to make God happy?" What do they feel they have to do to be a child of God? What does God expect before he accepts them?

The concept of grace is a difficult one to accept. It always seems there should be a catch somewhere. Maybe that's why Paul had to keep repeating it, and so do we. God's gift is a free gift. Help the class talk through this idea and understand what it is God offers us in Jesus Christ. He offers us full forgiveness and his boundless love. This is what Paul was so excited about, and it's certainly just as important for us as it was for Paul's day.

In their notebooks, your students should write a paragraph about this letter to the Galatians. They should briefly summarize what the book is about. Have them make use of terms such as *Christian freedom, law,* and *grace* as a way of reviewing Paul's emphasis.

In closing, review your list of New Testament titles found on the board. What general things have we learned about epistles? Then briefly restate the following points for the benefit of their notebooks:

1. Paul wrote letters when he had something important to say about a theological problem. They were written to specific people or congregations about specific needs.

2. Paul's letter to Galatians gave him a chance to proclaim what he considered to be a central concept for Christians—that in Jesus Christ, God has done everything necessary for our salvation.

3. This message was important for Christians who worried about keeping the law and trying to qualify for God's love. This concept is equally important for us today because our human tendency is to think in terms of what we have to do in order to merit his love.

Closing prayer

Ask the group to give sentence prayers about what God's grace means for their lives. You can close with a sentence when everyone has had an opportunity to participate.

Home assignment

Ask the students to carefully read the material in Chapter 30 and the biblical material assigned with it.

Objective

The purpose of this lesson is to restate Paul's theme of grace—that God has reached out in love and made us his own. Just as he promised Abraham that he would bless him and his children, so he promises us that we are his chosen people. All Abraham had to do was trust God to keep his word. That's all we have to do, too.

Biblical basis

Galatians 3–4

Background information

We are using two chapters to study this central concept of grace. It's important to remember that we have to understand this in order to understand the New Testament. God keeps all the promises he makes. He is consistent in his gracious and loving concern for people.

There may be things that you were unable to complete in the last lesson, especially questions about the purpose of the law and how we can live as Christians if we don't earn God's love. This lesson gives another opportunity to work on the answers.

Be careful to avoid the idea that the Old Testament is law and the New Testament is gospel. Chapter 30 points out that God made promises to Abraham, and Abraham followed him and trusted him on that basis. That was long before the law came into being. The whole story in the Old and New Testaments is one of God's consistent and loving nature toward us. The words *trust* and *faith* are key words. They describe how Abraham reacted to God's promises. We have to trust God and take him at his word, too. A commentary on Galatians would be helpful for your own understanding of what Paul is saying here.

And be sure to review the Old Testament chapters about Abraham and the covenant. You might want to use some of this in class. If not, at least refresh your own memory about Abraham and his faith in God's promises.

Preparation for class

Pictures of Abraham and the chart of Abraham and his descendants will be helpful links in helping your students see the idea of faith as being the key to God's plan.

The following optional activities might help your class visualize the grace and faith concept we're talking about:

1. Consider making a grace mobile using important words and ideas from the study. Bring to class materials that can be used by the students—such as posterboard, colored construction paper, wire hangers or lightweight wire, black thread, needles, and felt-tip markers in various colors. Construct your own mobile in advance and use it as a focal point for your students as they arrive. Then let them use their own ideas to make their own.

2. Creative writing is another way of encouraging individual students to express their ideas. Provide paper and pencils and ask them to write poetry, short stories, or journal kinds of material. The subject should be that God's love comes to us freely, through Jesus Christ, because he loves us and keeps his promises. He calls us to trust him.

The lesson experience

Begin the class with prayer. As your students arrive, review some of the ideas from last week's chapter. Get them thinking about some of the key words of the last chapter—*faith, truth, gospel, grace, law, free.* When everyone is ready, suggest praying about what we have learned in these last weeks concerning God's love and acceptance.

30

Who Can You Trust?

Briefly review the main ideas of Chapter 29 in which we were introduced to Paul's letters, and particularly to Galatians. Who can find Galatia on the map? Why was Paul writing to these people? The first two chapters included a defense of himself. Why did Paul find this necessary? What was the main idea Paul was trying to get across? Try to put this in one sentence.

Give your class a few minutes to review their reading assignment and their notes from last week.

Write the word *theologian* on the board. Can your students give a definition of the word? Write their suggestions on the board, too. Then explain its meaning, using a dictionary, and write it on the board, pointing out the parts of the word—*theo* (God) and *logy* (study of). Why would we call Paul a theologian?

Have your students heard anything about Pharisees before? What can they remember about them? Try to emphasize their training in the law and in the interpretation of Scripture, rather than merely their criticism of Jesus. They criticized Jesus because he claimed to be the fulfillment of the law. Talk about what it meant for Paul to be a Pharisee and how useful his training was for him in the role he now played in the church. He was not writing stories for children. He wanted to challenge the Galatians to think and grow in their new Christian faith.

In this session we study Chapters 3 and 4 of Galatians. Have the class turn to Chapter 3 and notice that Paul begins with an Old Testament history lesson. Does your class have any idea why he would do this?

Paul probably wanted to let the Galatians know he understood the Old Testament better than many of his opponents who were doing all the talking about keeping the law. And he insisted that the best way to understand Jesus was to study the Old Testament.

Does this seem strange to your class? We sometimes make the mistake of thinking of the Old Testament and everything that went before Jesus as law, and everything after him as gospel. But the lesson Paul gives us here is clear. Abraham trusted God. All he had was his faith in God. From the very beginning God's relationship to his chosen people was based on faith. And Paul declares that God blesses all the people on earth on that same basis. Reread Gal. 3:15-18 together.

But what's the purpose of the law then? Read Gal. 3:19-20 aloud. God's people needed help and guidance until the promise was fulfilled. The law is a good word, but not the last word. In many ways, it's still the best guide we have to what is right and wrong. (Remember our study of civil law and its basis in the commandments?) Especially, it shows us our need of a Savior. Can your class rephrase the purpose of the law in their own words? Can they write it in one sentence in their notebooks?

Have your class read Gal. 3:28-29. Ask them to discuss the chapter's focus on Christ as God's way of making all of us his: Jew and Greek, slave and free, male and female. All who trust in Jesus have inherited God's original promise to Abraham. Since the promise is for everyone, the old restrictions have been dropped. We are heirs to that first promise at the beginning of our story!

Growing up. In Chapter 4 of Galatians, Paul presents some arguments for the Galatians and for us about growing up and living in faith. Before we take a look at those arguments, let's review the idea of the advantages of being a baby.

Ask the students to respond to the paragraphs in the chapter about being a baby. It can be a soft life in many ways. But how do they think they would like it now? Would they like to return to being a baby again, or do they want to grow up? What are the advantages and disadvantages of growing up? Write a few of their ideas on the board, helping them to see what they feel are good and bad things about being a baby and about growing up.

Paul is not interested in giving the Galatians their choice. His opinion is that Christians should grow up, painful as that may be. Here are his arguments:

1. In Gal. 4:1-7, Paul explains what it's like to grow up. When you are young, you're under a guardian (the law), but when you grow up, you make decisions for yourself. Your guardian is not necessary in the same sense.

2. In Gal. 4:8-11, Paul attacks superstition and weakness. These people were afraid to trust God. They were looking for a rule book to follow.

3. In Gal. 4:12-20, Paul gives a personal plea. He expresses his concern and asks them to remember what they've been through together.

4. The allegory he tells in Gal. 4:21-31 is stretching the Genesis account and Paul knows it. This allegory in which each part of the story symbolizes something, is his way of trying again to make his point. God wants us to live in relationship with him; he's made a promise about it and he keeps his promises.

When you have completed the Bible study and the discussion of Paul's emphases, try to answer any remaining questions about this letter to the people in Galatia. Or any questions concerning the main ideas of grace, faith, and our relationship to God through Christ.

Work on projects. With the time remaining, choose one of the optional projects and give your students a chance to express in visual or written form what these two lessons are about.

1. If you choose the mobile, make sure the students understand they are to use simple words that have been talked about in a meaningful way, or symbols for those words that they can think of as being appropriate. Give them freedom to create their own version of the mobile, pointing out how each word is attached, dependent and connected to the others.

2. If you choose creative writing, describe the kinds of things you are interested in having them do. Explain that their original poetry need not rhyme and can be very simple, but it should express their own individuality. A diary or journal is a way of recording personal impressions of what Paul has said.

Try to give individual attention and help as your students are working on their projects. It's important to be supportive and helpful; everyone's work should be acceptable if it is honest and the result of thought and work. Students should not compete in such a project, but should work at expressing their own ideas and response to the lesson material.

Home assignment

Ask each student to read Chapter 31 and the biblical material before coming to class next week. If you are planning an exam for the last session, let your students know about it so they can plan and prepare. Tell them that you will review with them next week. Make sure any incomplete assignments are being done. Notebooks should be checked next week, too, to give your students an opportunity to complete them and bring them up to date.

31

Free! Free! Free!

Objective
The purpose of this lesson is for the student to take a look at Christian freedom and the responsibilities which accompany this freedom. As Christians we have been set free. We obey God and his law, not out of fear, but out of love, because we know of God's love for us in Jesus Christ.

Biblical basis
Galatians 5–6

Background information
This chapter is an opportunity to discuss many things. You may want to review some of the initial work you did last week on the idea of Christian freedom as found in Paul's letter to the Galatians. Remember Abraham. All those who trust in Christ have inherited God's promise to Abraham.

You might want to consider the role of good works in our Christian lives. Does God expect good works from us? Yes he does. But why should we do such things if we are free? Martin Luther would answer that if we are people of faith, then our faith will result in good works or, in other words, love for our neighbor. Our very freedom makes it possible for us to love and serve others.

The map of Paul's travels should be used to show and discuss how he was impelled by the Holy Spirit to keep moving, proclaiming the good news to everyone he could. Paul and his followers moved throughout the world of their day, planting the seeds of the gospel of Jesus Christ. Remember again how their witness started in Jerusalem and spread to all the world.

Think a bit about freedom. Freedom is a great responsibility for us Christians. We are called to love and serve others. Think of what this means for our affluent lives and the needs of those around us. Think of their poverty of mind and body and spirit. We who have been freed by Christ need to hear God's command to love our neighbor.

Preparation for class
Just one more chapter follows this one. You may want to use some of your time to review the year, tying together any loose ends and preparing your class for a final exam if you plan to give one. Practice your freedom by showing your love and letting your students know how much you have appreciated them during this year.

Plan something special for the class to do together as a sort of celebration! You could have it this week, or at the final class meeting. It need not be elaborate, but it should involve the class in some activity which will give them a chance to celebrate each other and the year they have spent together.

You could plan any of the following:

1. A popcorn party in which students share what they liked about the class.

2. A review to prepare for the test, written by class members, done as a contest in teams. Provide treats following the contest.

3. A film about a young Christian who learns to make decisions and develops a life-style based on freedom and responsibility.

4. A creative time of preparing "gift" packages for the other class members. The gift should tell something good about that person.

Keep a map of Paul's missionary journeys on your bulletin board, so you can talk about his travels during this session.

If there is to be an exam, announce it during this session. Allow time for review, send sample questions home, or give your students a chance to write their own test questions during class. They could try them out on each other. They should know how much time they have for the test, what kinds of questions they can expect, and how they can best prepare for it. It could cover material from the whole year, or be a unit test on what has been covered since the last exam.

The lesson experience

As the students arrive, begin looking over their notebooks. Each student should have a chance to talk with you about the notebook, what has been put in it, and how it has helped in learning. You, in turn, can comment on what you see there. This checkup is an opportunity for you to talk with each person about what has happened during the year. You can learn a great deal from the notebook.

This is also an opportunity for you to thank each student for his or her participation in the course. Give a personal word of support and appreciation for the relationships that have developed and for the work God's Spirit has done with the class during the year.

Other students can use this time to review their chapter and the biblical material in it. When they have completed this, they can begin reviewing material to be covered in the exam, writing questions about important points in each chapter, and answering those questions.

Discussing the chapter. Begin by asking some questions to review what you learned about Paul's letter to the Galatians from the last lesson. What problems did the Galatians have? What did Paul say about their problems? And how did he deal with them? He had much to say about the law. Can you remember some of his points?

In this chapter we are still studying the letter to the Galatians. Can you summarize in a sentence or two what Paul is saying in Chapters 5 and 6? What are some of the main words he uses? Is there one word which keeps coming up again and again? What about the words "Christ" and "free"? Write these words on the board. What is their significance—what does Paul say about them? Review the chapter together, talking about freedom and what it means for a Christian to be free. What is Paul trying to point out in his argument about circumcision? Look at Gal. 5:3-6. Would Paul be against our practice of circumcising baby boys today? What is he saying here?

If a Christian is free, can he do anything he wants to do? It seems as if Paul is saying we can do anything we please. Is that true? Read Gal. 5:13-25 together. How are we to understand this kind of freedom and responsibility?

Look at the example in our chapter about the two teenagers. What is the difference in their decisions? Our reasons for doing things are important. Paul is saying that motives count. Christians obey not out of fear, but out of love.

Role playing. This could be a good time to involve your students in some role playing about the freedom and responsibility they have as Christians. Divide the class into teams of four or five students, assigning the roles or letting them make up their own.

Give them some time to discuss and practice what they want to do. Have them do their role playing, and then let them share their impressions of each one. The idea of role playing is to try to put themselves in the situation they are acting out. How would they have reacted? What was right or wrong about it? What things had to be considered?

Possible situations for role playing:

1. A group of young people have access to some beer. They can get it free and have to decide if they should drink it. Some do, some don't. Those that don't have different reasons for refusing. Discuss reasons for drinking it and for refusing.

2. Three girls are talking about shoplifting. One girl decides to take a sweater and asks the others to take one, too. Show what they must consider before they act, what they would say and do, and what the first girl will say and do if the others turn her down.

3. Cheating on tests in math has been the topic for discussion by two boys. One is a good math student, the other only average. What would they be saying to each other? Make up a conversation and show what happens to them as they decide what to do.

4. A boy and his parents are having a discussion about why he came home so late. The boy feels he is free to come and go as he pleases. The parents feel they should set time limits for him. What should all three consider and what happens?

5. A family is taking a vacation. They are deciding about whether they should plan to worship while they're gone. What would they talk about and what is the result?

After the situations have been presented and discussed, spend some time talking about the idea that church people are not perfect. Some people have suggested that Christians have to be perfect. Where do your students think this idea that church people should be perfect originates? Could it be that we still sometimes act as if we had to earn God's love—as if we actually could?

Do Christians still make mistakes? Are your students aware of some of these mistakes? Why do we keep making mistakes? What can we learn from this?

Help your students talk about our human weakness and inability to do right, even though we try. We live in a broken world and we will continue to have the problem of sin. No one is exempt.

This gives us insight into why God is the one to depend on and trust. No matter how hard we try to do right, we can't do it—but God can. His love and forgiveness as shown in Jesus Christ is the answer to all our mistakes. Paul knew this, and he proclaimed it to the Galatians in Chapter 6. He didn't expect perfection. He reminded the Galatians (and us) to care for each other and to be gentle with those who make mistakes. God comes to us where we are with his love. His kingdom is present among us even though we are not perfect.

Course review. This is probably the time for review. This year has involved a telling and a retelling of the story of God and his love for his people, his promises, and how he keeps those promises in the coming of Jesus Christ. The story goes on. As the students begin to put the review together, remind them that the story is a continuing one and that it is still going on. We are as much a part of it as Abraham, Moses, and Paul.

Decide what form of review will work best for your class. You might pair off in twos, assigning several chapters to each pair, asking them to review it in the reading book and their own notebooks, and then to write six questions on the most important ideas in those chapters.

The class could share their questions in several ways. You could collect them and have them duplicated for next week's session, or each group could read theirs aloud as the others write them down.

A contest using the students' review questions could be fun, too. Divide your class into two teams. Then line them up facing each other. You read the questions to members of each team, one at a time. If one team fails to answer, the other team has a turn. If they get it right, their team scores a point. The team with the most points at the end wins. This would give your class an opportunity to hear the questions and answers in the review. The competitive spirit also provides a challenge to study for the exam and can be fun.

Options. You might choose to show a film at this point. Look for a film that zeroes in on decision making, Christian freedom, and responsibility. Introduce the film before you show it and give a few hints of things to watch for. Then allow time after the showing to discuss and relate it to Galatians. What happens in our lives as we come to understand freedom and responsibility?

Another option is a popcorn party. Consider it if your final session will be busy with review, exam, etc. This might be a good time to celebrate the opportunities you've had together and the relationships that have developed among class members. Share a treat and some conversation about the group, what you have come to appreciate about each other, and how you have grown together.

A final option is the preparation of "gift" packages. Details for this optional activity are found in Chapter 32.

Home assignment

Ask each student to read Chapter 32 and the biblical material in it, and to prepare for the exam if you are planning to give one.

Paul's World

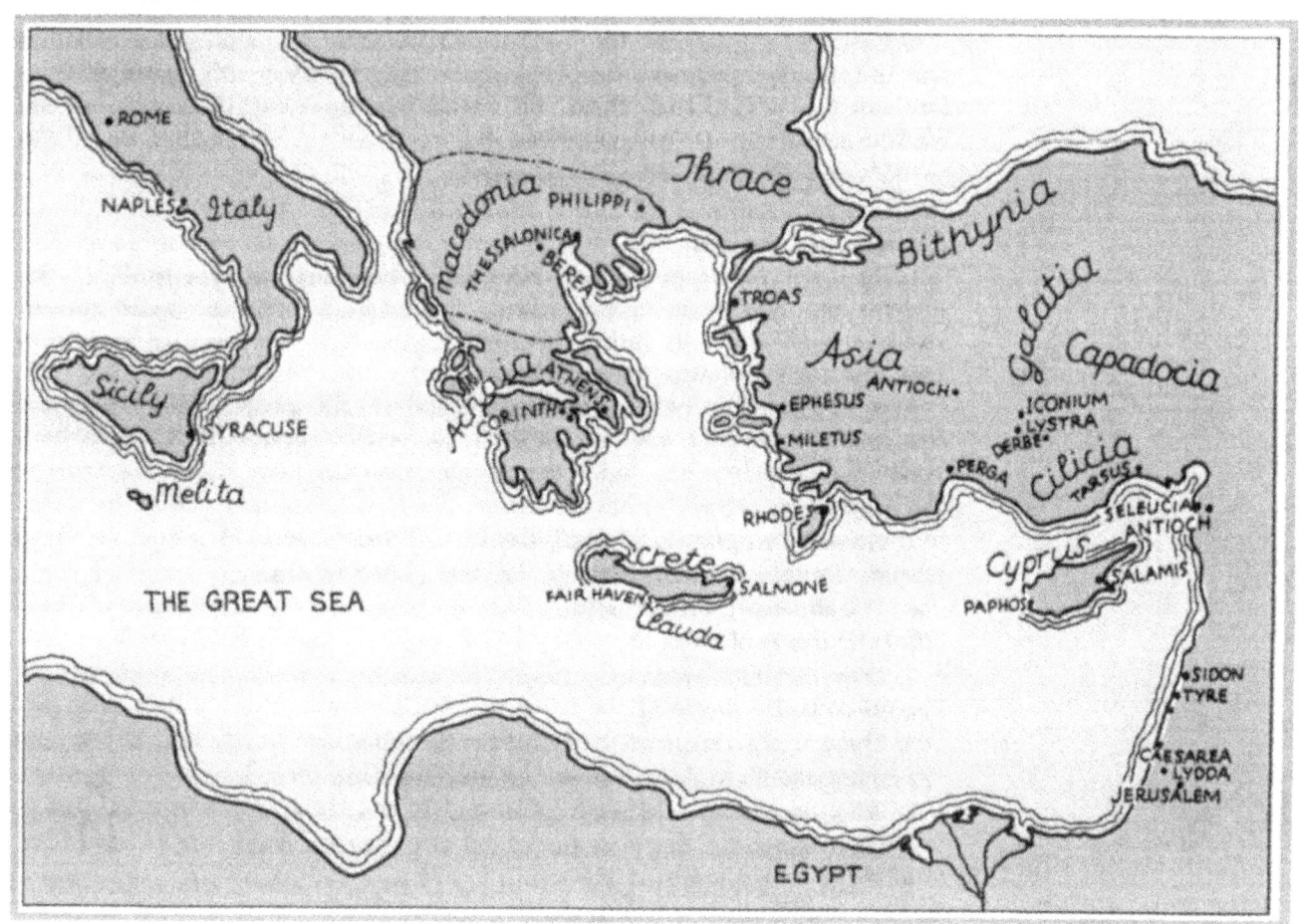

The End?

Objective
The purpose of this lesson is to study the message of hope as found in the Revelation to John. We have been studying events of the past: God's choosing a people and his working through them. In this lesson we are reminded that with God there is a future too. The future belongs to him just as the past and present do. When we know this, we can live in hope.

Biblical basis
Revelation 1:1-20; 21:1—22:21

Background information
Many people in our day feel there is no future. They question the purpose of life and whether or not the human race has a future. There is disillusionment. When the world around looks bleak, then the future seems hopeless, and people despair.

Our Christian hope is that we trust the future to God. We have seen him at work in history keeping his promises to his people. We know that his kingdom is forever. We know this because of the death and resurrection of our Lord Jesus Christ. Because he lives, we live, now and forever. The darkness within and without does not have the final word. God has the final word. We live in hope.

As Christians we do not need to know when and how Christ will come again. We dare to live today, trusting the future to him. The purpose of the book of Revelation is not to give us some kind of timetable for the end of the world. We read it for the same kind of message of hope and comfort that it gave to Christians in the early church who faced pressures, torture, and disillusionment. It reminded them, as it reminds us, that Jesus is Lord, even over death. Nothing can change that. The final victory is his.

Review the chapter and the biblical material from Revelation, remembering that this was the good news for people who were struggling with powerful forces that threatened to destroy them. No matter how terrifying life might become for them, God was in charge and one day would set up his kingdom for all the world to see. This truth remains unchanged.

Preparation for class
If there are notebooks that you have still not checked, be sure to do so. Remember the importance of commenting and complimenting in regard to your students and their work. And of course, Chapter 32 is important, so be sure to give it enough attention during this session.

A brief review of the year could be a part of this session. Use of the time line may be a helpful way to review. A quiz over Chapters 29-32 would be a good way to review; you could use the quiz included here. Check the answers in class if there is time.

1. Name two cities that have books of the New Testament named for them (*Rome, Corinth, Ephesus, Philippi, Colossae, Thessalonica*).

2. Which were probably written first; the gospels or the early letters of Paul? (*the early letters of Paul*).

3. Why did Paul write the epistles? (*He usually wrote to help people or congregations with a problem*).

4. What is the theme of the letter to the Galatians? (*God's love is free and for everybody; it's a declaration of Christian freedom*).

5. What one word does Paul use to describe God's great love for us? (*grace*).

6. What does the word "theology" mean? (*a study of God*).

7. What responsibilities grow out of our Christian freedom? (*the responsibility to love and to serve our neighbor*).

8. Who kept Paul going in the face of harassment and imprisonment? *(the Holy Spirit)*.

9. What is the Revelation to John about? *(the last things, hope)*.

10. What's most important to remember about the coming end of this world? *(Jesus has triumphed; God is in charge)*.

A celebration of some sort was mentioned in the last lesson. If you didn't get to it in the last session, allow time in this period just to enjoy being together for this final time.

An optional activity could be the preparation of the "gift" packages for each student. If you intend to do this, bring enough envelopes and index cards so each student can write one out for each classmate. If you have 10 students, you would need nine envelopes and nine index cards for each student.

The lesson experience

Begin your class with this: "We have been following the story of God and his people for 32 sessions. How would you write the ending to the story?" Give the students a few minutes to write a paragraph about how God will end the world, what will happen to everybody, and anything they feel important to include about the end of the story. Ask them to share what they have written. Where did they get their ideas? Did they think about this week's chapter? It says a number of things about the end.

Getting into the chapter. Give your students a minute to review Chapter 32. Begin discussion of it by asking them to describe what the Bible says will happen at the end. As they talk about this, jot some of the things on the board. Why is the question mark included in the title of this chapter? What do they remember from Chapter 32 about the Revelation to John? What was it and when was it written? To whom? And most important, why?

Give students the opportunity to suggest answers to some of these questions and to raise any of their own. Discuss the significance of the images used. What does the chapter tell about them? They may be especially interested in the code names for Roman emperors and others who were trying to eliminate the Christians. Why did John write to the seven churches using this kind of code language?

It is important that they get an idea of the ending as described in the book of Revelation. The last two chapters leave no doubt about who is in charge. The final act belongs to God! What does the class think about the description of heaven? What is their idea of how things should turn out in the end? Discuss the ending they wrote for the story.

When can we expect the end? Some groups have tried to predict when this would happen. Are you acquainted with such groups? Stress that only God knows when this will happen and how, but we need not waste our time worrying or guessing. All we need to know is that he has chosen us and nothing can change that.

Evaluation. At this point it would be helpful to give your students an opportunity to evaluate what has happened. You might want them to write a paragraph or two about the class, the people in it, the things you did, the book and the course, and whatever they found important to them during this study. Ask them to be honest and thoughtful. Give them time to think about the experience and to write their feelings. These should not be shared, but the students should be encouraged to express their own opinions and feelings about what has happened.

Caring for each other. Since this is your last session, use a few minutes for a sharing and caring kind of project. The point of this activity is to have each student consider and care for other students in the class. Throughout the year we have tried to build relationships with one another in order to become a concerned and caring group. We have talked about acceptance and love for one another, and we have tried to practice it in activities and in our experiences with each other.

Each person in the class brought some unique gifts and qualities to the class. Each is an important person. And so each student is to write on an index card a message to each of the other class members. It is to be personal—about that person specifically. It is to be positive—something good that you remember happening or you noticed about the person. And it is to be private—something for that person to read and not necessarily to share with others. Each may write whatever he or she wants and then put the card in an envelope with the person's name on it. Do this for each class member.

When all the "gifts" are ready, the teacher should collect them. As the students leave, their packets of envelopes are given to them to take home, a reminder of the relationships and experiences that have just been completed.

Closing prayer

By this time your students should be equipped with all kinds of ideas about prayer. Suggest they each try to contribute to a ring prayer. Have the class form a circle, holding hands, and begin the prayer with the person on your right. When the first prayer is completed that person squeezes the hand of the individual on his or her right, who prays in turn, and so on. You will be the last person, closing the prayer with thanksgiving for the presence and growth of each class member and praising God for his many blessings during the year.

Individualized Instruction

Introduction

Many congregations are interested in a different approach to teaching from the traditional classroom teaching methods suggested in this guide. Some pastors and teachers have a wealth of ideas with which they want to experiment. They recognize that each student is unique and that there are as many different ways of learning as there are students in a class.

Individualized instruction is a classroom approach that gives the individual student more responsibility for shaping his or her own learning experiences, and it seeks to reflect the unique needs and abilities of each learner. In order to help those who have an interest in pursuing an individualized instruction experience, this section is included as a resource. Its aim is to give you a starting point for using your own ideas and plans.

A *learning contract* is one way of individualizing the instruction a student gets. To arrive at a contract for each student, the teacher and student together agree on the goals the student will work toward. Then they decide on what learning activities or experiences the student will use in reaching those goals. This is what goes into the learning contract that a student makes with the teacher. A model learning contract will be provided for the first division of the material of this course; then resources and projects will be suggested for the remaining chapters of the book.

This material will give you an idea of how to set up individual contracts according to the needs and interests of your students. It will also leave you free to develop your own style of contract, rather than impose on you a plan for each student.

To help make the most of this type of program, we suggest you keep in mind some guidelines for individualized instruction:

1. Explain to each student and to the parents just what you are planning and why you are using this method of instruction.

2. Agree together with the student that he or she has the main responsibility for learning. You will help with resources, questions, and supportive involvement.

3. Consider the interests, needs, and abilities of your students as you draw up any contract for learning. Consult with them as you present the contract and talk about the work to be done on it.

4. Involve yourself with the student as the work is being done. Although you are not lecturing, you can be helpful by providing guidance, materials, resources, and encouragement.

5. Follow up on contracts made, helping students who might misunderstand or have difficulty getting started. Be there to answer questions, to encourage the quick learner, to show patience with problems.

6. Fulfillment of a contract is a time for sharing together what has been learned. It is a time to evaluate learning, and also a time when both teacher and student can take pride in accomplishment and creativity.

Good individualized instruction provides a framework in which the student has both flexibility and direction. It gets the person actively involved in learning, and allows freedom and creativity. It can be an exciting adventure to learn in this way. Try your own ideas and be sure to allow your students to try theirs.

Model for learning contract

Learning contract: Old Testament Study—Unit 1, Chapters 1-5

Material to be covered:
- The introduction to the study of the Bible
- The early story of God and his people in relation to Abraham and his sons

Theme

The Bible is the story of God and his people. It reveals in both a divine and a human way a God who loves his people and keeps his promises, even when his people are not perfect.

Objective

The aim of this contract is to help the student understand that God is a God of love, and that the story of the Bible is the story of God and his people. It is also important for the student to realize that he is a part of this same story. God continues to promise us good things. He is faithful to us even when we make mistakes.

Contract agreement

Upon completing this contract, the learner should be able to do the following:

1. Write a four-page essay on the Bible, including a discussion of its being divine and human, an explanation and examples of the diversity in the Bible, and some word on the main theme of the Bible.

2. List the three parts of the promise that God made to Abraham and discuss what it meant that God made such a promise to his people and what we learn about God from this covenant relationship.

In addition to the above, the learner may select at least three of the following, and can add original projects with the consent of the teacher:

1. Create an art project depicting the idea of the creation story. It might be a collage, mural, drawing, or bulletin board.

2. Use an Old Testament map to trace the journeys of Abraham as God calls him and leads him to the land of promise.

3. Make a list of the things that went wrong when man disobeyed God in the story of Adam and Eve.

4. Draw a family tree of Abraham and his descendants.

5. Name and give examples of three different kinds of writing in the Bible.

6. Discuss the biblical story of creation, and whether this story is in conflict with scientific accounts.

Suggested activities for subunits

For the purpose of showing the adaptability of this course to an individualized approach, Unit 1 (Chapters 1-5) has been divided into three subunits of one or two chapters each. What follows is a list of learning activities suggested for each subunit in Unit 1.

1. "The Story of God's Love, Part 1"

1. Read Chapter 1 of the reading book. Study the Bible books listed in the front of your Bible.

2. Make a list of the kinds of writing that are in the Bible, trying to give examples of each type as you go along.

3. Write in your own words in what way the Bible is divine, and in what way it is human.

4. Share with your teacher in just a few sentences what you think the theme of the Bible is.

2. "Covenant and Faith"

1. Read Chapter 2 of the reading book and the biblical material included in it. Read Chapter 5 and the biblical material.

2. Draw a map of the Old Testament world, using a good Bible atlas. Using an encyclopedia, find out what the Fertile Crescent was and how it affected life at that time. Trace the journeys of Abraham on the map. Then talk with two other students about why the route he took was good or bad for that time.

3. Find out what you can about the state of Israel today. Look up the words Palestine and Canaan and compare information about modern Israel with the historical development of God's promised land to Abraham.

4. Write a paragraph about what it means to be chosen by God. How does he choose his people? Why does he choose some and not others? What does he expect of his people?

5. Trace God's continuing promise through Abraham's descendants. Talk with your teacher or another student about how the promise continued, why certain children became next in line, and who they were. What kind of people does God work through?

6. Explain the word *covenant*. What does it mean in terms of the promise made to Abraham and in terms of the promise God makes to us?

3. "Creation and the Fall"

1. Read Chapters 3 and 4 and the biblical material assigned for those two chapters.

2. Write a paragraph about why the creation story is included in the Bible and what the main theme of that story is.

3. Talk to three or four other students and your teacher about the biblical story of creation. Discuss how you feel about that story and about what you've studied in school regarding the beginning of the world.

4. Make a list of things giving evidence that man has not lived up to his responsibility to take care of God's creation. What environmental problems do we have that relate to this?

5. Using your chapters and your Bible, write a page about what went wrong. How did God's creation get so messed up? Whose fault is it? What things happened that show man continued to do wrong?

6. Be part of a small group discussing the need for making decisions and choosing right and wrong in daily life. Try to include some of these questions:

    Whose idea was it to give us freedom of choice?
    Who is responsible for doing right or wrong? The individual? Society? God?
    What is involved in the decisions we make?
    Why doesn't God just decide things for us?

Additional activities

Other creative possibilities may come to your mind. Feel free to explore topics and characters which interest you, or to do a project that is not suggested as part of this contract. Arrange with your teacher to include these as part of this unit of study. Here are some ideas:

1. Study the Arab people and their beginnings with Hagar and Ishmael. Relate it to the modern Arab and Jewish troubles.

2. Develop a character study on one of the people in these stories, keeping in mind the idea that God chose them for his purposes. What are they like? What problems do they have?

3. Talk with a family who have recently moved to your community from another country or part of the country. Write a report about their move, their problems in adjustment, their feelings of loneliness,

and their family reactions. Relate it to Abraham and his family move.

Other learning contracts

The model learning contract shown above for Unit 1, Chapters 1-5, is an example of how such a contract can be drawn up. You will have ideas of your own about what should be included in these contracts and can use whatever part of this model is practical for your students. Following are suggested unit divisions for the rest of the course, with some ideas for contract projects. You can add to these in the light of your own ideas and expectations.

Suggested unit divisions for individualization

Old Testament		New Testament	
Unit 1	Chapters 1-5	Unit 5	Chapters 17-19
Unit 2	Chapters 6-9	Unit 6	Chapters 20-24
Unit 3	Chapters 10-13	Unit 7	Chapters 25-28
Unit 4	Chapters 14-16		(Chapter 28 could also be moved into Unit 4)
		Unit 8	Chapters 29-32

Suggested unit activities

Unit 2   Chapters 6-9

This unit covers the exodus, the story of Moses and the giving of the law, the conquest of the promised land, the judges, and the beginning of kingship.

Contract agreement suggestions:

1. Write a theme about Moses and his life with the people of Israel. Include contributions he made to their deliverance, his encounters with God, and the giving of the law.

2. Make a scrapbook entitled, "Judges and Kings of Israel." Include a description of each of the six judges and the three kings mentioned in the reading book. Add symbols or a drawing for each of them.

In addition, choose two or three of the following project suggestions:

1. Rewrite the Ten Commandments in your own words. Use Luther's Small Catechism for ideas. Explain the meaning of the commandments for your life.

2. Make a TV box like the one described in Chapter 8. Depict the conquest of the promised land and the establishment of the nation of Israel, including the material on the judges.

3. Draw a mural about the beginning of kingship, portraying Saul, David, Solomon, and the prophets who lived at that time. Include the personalities and important events or contributions of each.

4. Plan a panel discussion about the law today. Invite people from your school, the police department, or your government to discuss how laws are made and enforced. Write a brief summary of the discussion.

5. Discuss with your teacher what you consider to be the most important events and characters of this unit, why you feel they should be studied, and how they fit into the story of God and his people.

Unit 3   Chapters 10-13

This unit covers the division of the kingdom, the prophets of repentance, the exile, and the prophets of promise and hope.

Contract agreement suggestions:

1. Make a repentance cycle depicting the role of the prophets and how they brought about change. Show how it applies to your own life decisions.

2. Study the exile of an individual or some group of people. Write a two-page paper describing the circumstances of the exile, the move, the adjustments, and the feelings involved. Include your own feelings about how people adjust when they move from place to place.

In addition, select two or three of the following project suggestions:

1. Do a biblical study of the prophets, using Chapters 11 and 13 as a starting point. Try to find out who they were, how they became prophets, how God worked through them, and some of the contributions they made to the people of Israel. Discuss this with your teacher.

2. Make a map of the kingdom of Israel before and after the division. Trace the movement of the people of God into exile. Include important nations, cities, and other geographical places that are mentioned in your study.

3. Write a prophecy as though you were a modern-day prophet, warning people about their wrong activities and attitudes and what they should do about them, and what will happen if they do not change. Share your feelings about this writing with a small group of students.

4. Make up a test for this unit of study. Include questions about the divided kingdom, the prophets, the exile, and the continuing story of God's people. Give it to at least four people and then discuss it with them.

Unit 4   Chapters 14-16

This unit covers the return from exile and the intertestamental period.

Contract agreement suggestions:

1. Write an essay about the return from exile, important accomplishments that took place then, and the problems that arose after the return.

2. Write a song or a psalm about yourself and your feelings about God. Include how you feel about him and his story and about yourself.

In addition, choose two or three of the following:

1. Research the Apocrypha at the library. Find a few Bibles containing the Apocrypha. Present a two-minute talk to the class about these books, how they came to be included in some Bibles and excluded from others, and what we know about them and their importance to our story.

2. Study the books of Ruth or Jonah. What does this story tell us about who God is, what he is like, and what it is like to be a human being.

3. Make a collage of words and pictures which depict the human response we find described in Chapter 15, especially feelings and experiences people have and how they let God know what is happening to them.

4. Make a replica of the temple as part of a research project on the rebuilding that took place after the return from exile. You will find information in Chapter 14, the Bible, and a Bible dictionary. Show the replica to your class and explain why it is built as it is.

5. Discuss legalism with your teacher after reading either Jonah or Ruth. What do these stories tell us about narrowness; why might they have been written? What application do they have to our lives today?

Unit 5   Chapters 17-19

This unit introduces the story of Jesus. The central event is the cross and resurrection. It is this central event that is at the heart of the entire story of God and his people.

Contract agreement suggestions:

1. Make a time line like the one found in Chapter 17 and a one-page report explaining the importance of time in the writing of the New Testament. What is the reason for the order of the books as we find them in the New Testament?

2. Write a poem or essay about Jesus' death and resurrection. What did it mean to his followers at the time? What does it mean to you personally?

In addition, choose two or three of the following project suggestions:

1. Listen to the record, *Jesus Christ Superstar*, and write a one-page comment on what you think the central message of its music and lyrics is.

2. Make an Easter banner using symbols and words which you think would lead people to do some serious thinking about the meaning of Easter.

3. Write an Easter sunrise service or a Good Friday service for your church. Include how you would want the church to look, the colors to be used, a short sermon, Bible texts, hymns and songs, and whatever other ideas you think would make a meaningful service. Describe your service to a group of students.

4. Make a chart of the Old and New Testaments, listing the books in each and the kinds of writing found in each. Discuss the similarities and the differences in the two parts of Scripture, telling what the main theme in each is.

5. Interview your pastor or a funeral director concerning their ideas about death and their experiences with it. Write a two-page report on what is said. Share it with your teacher.

6. Write your own will. Give some thought to what you have to give away, what things you want done after you die, things you wish to say to people, etc. Talk about this privately with one other person: parent, teacher, or some close friend.

Unit 6   Chapters 20-24

This unit covers the ministry of Jesus from his baptism to Palm Sunday. It includes lessons on his miracles and his teaching in parables. It discusses the calling of the disciples and the plans Jesus had for them.

Contract agreement suggestions:

1. Study the miracles of Jesus as discussed in Chapter 21. Either write a poem about how he used miracles or a report about what they were meant to do. Include some details about what happened and the effect it had on people.

2. Write a one-page theme on "Who Jesus is to me." First study Chapter 23 and the biblical material assigned in it. What did people find him to be? What did he mean to different people?

In addition, choose two or three of the following project suggestions:

1. Attend a church council meeting or arrange to talk with several council members. What do they see as the work of the council and the task of the church? Talk with them about the material in Chapter 24. What is your congregation doing to fulfill the tasks Jesus gave his followers? Discuss this with your teacher.

2. Do an art piece on John the Baptist. Review the material in Chapter 20 and do further research in the Bible. Choose a mural, collage, banner, mobile, sculpture, or picture to depict his life or his message.

3. Report on a favorite teacher as described in Chapter 22. Report on Jesus as a teacher after studying that material. What qualities do you find in a good teacher?

4. Write a modern-day parable by taking one of the parables in Chapter 22 and updating it, using people, situations, and places that occur in life now. Be sure to have a main point to the parable.

5. Write a letter home as though you were the lost son in Chapter 22. Describe what happened to you when you left home, how you feel now, and ask to come back. Use modern places, people, and things.

Unit 7   Chapters 25-28

This unit covers the story of Jesus' entry into Jerusalem, Pentecost, the early witness of the disciples, and the beginning of Paul's story.

Contract agreement suggestions:

1. Make a banner for the celebration of Pentecost. Write a paragraph explaining this day and what it means in the story of God's people.

2. Plan a witnessing activity where you have an opportunity to proclaim what you believe about Jesus and the church to someone in need of a visit. If you can, include others in this plan.

In addition, choose two or three of the following project suggestions:

1. Plan a birthday party in honor of the church's birthday, Pentecost. Think of ways your church could celebrate this festival and present your ideas to your pastor or church council.

2. Write a research report on the book of Acts. Read student book Chapter 26 first and then the entire book in the Bible. Add insights from a Bible commentary and report on the date, author, content, and theme.

3. Memorize Acts 1:7-8 and write a short paragraph on why this verse is important.

4. Complete the Scramble Graph in Chapter 26. Write the Bible verse, and then make a list of the extra words that have to do with Pentecost but are not part of the verse. Go over these with your teacher.

5. Study Martin Luther and the kind of witness he was at the time of the Reformation. Give a two-minute talk about his witness for Jesus to your class.

Unit 8   Chapters 29-32

This unit completes the course. We study the work of Paul and his fellow workers, focusing on Galatians. The theme is that of God's grace in Jesus Christ. He loves us and nothing can change that, not even the end of this world.

Contract agreement suggestions:

1. Write a character study of Paul, describing who he was, his training, and how he became a witness for Jesus Christ. How did God use him to spread the good news?

2. Make a mobile on the theme of grace after studying the material in Chapter 30. Depict in words and symbols the ideas Paul stressed to the Galatians about God's free gift of love in Jesus Christ.

In addition, choose two or three of the following project suggestions:

1. Draw a map which shows the world as it was in the time of Paul's travels, locating the cities and areas he visited.

2. Describe heaven as you envision it, comparing it to the description in Chapter 32 of Revelation. Talk to your teacher about your description and how you came to this idea.

3. Evaluate the course and write a one-page report on what you think was the main theme, the central characters and events, and the most important thing you learned.

4. Plan a display for the congregation about the people and events you have studied during this course. It might consist of pictures, symbols, maps, reports, banners, and a brief report or chart listing major characters and stories in the Bible.

5. Read the letter to the Galatians. Study Chapters 29-32 in our reading book, plus any commentaries or other biblical helps you can find. Then talk with a small group of students or your teacher about why Paul wrote this letter, its main content, and what you think it has to say to us today.

6. Prepare a debate with one other student on the subject of freedom and responsibility.

Retreats

Introduction

Before we go into detail about setting up a retreat schedule for using parts of this course material, it might be good to talk a little about retreats in general and to explain some of the things you will need to consider in planning one.

A retreat should be a "time apart"

A retreat is a special kind of experience which lends itself to building in-depth relationships, thought, reflection, and genuine enjoyment of life. There are opportunities for being together in a way you cannot duplicate in the classroom setting. Most teachers have found that retreats give rise to unstructured and unplanned learning. Spontaneous questions and "gab fests" produce real searching for meaning. Students can ask questions and make comments they seem uncomfortable with in the week by week study sessions. They sense that this is an informal time of sharing and being—a happening. You will want to plan your retreat in such a way as to take advantage of the students' natural "freeing up" in being away from home, in the informal setting, and in time together not planned for anything specific.

The schedule should be flexible

It is tempting to try to cover as much material as possible when you have your class "captive" for such an extended period of time in comparison to one or one and a half hours per week. Careful, though—the experience of being together and what happens between you as persons will be as much a learning and growing part of the retreat as the structured sessions of input, creative activity, etc. We sometimes feel time needs to be filled with particular activity directed at a lesson or related to it. But time spent being simply with one another, or time spent alone to reflect and enjoy life is equally important. If there is adequate opportunity for recreation, music, talking, and doing nothing, the scheduled sessions will be as welcome a change as going back to school after summer vacation.

Make the most of your setting

Wherever your retreat is held, it will be unlike your classroom in most cases. Capitalize on this fact and adapt to it rather than trying to get the retreat setting to be like a classroom. Casual discussions held while sitting on the floor or out-of-doors, eating and talking together, communion in an informal worship, can be exciting and stimulating changes from the usual sessions you have had.

Involve the class in planning

It will be a schedule more easily accepted if the students feel they have had a share in putting it together. You might let them share their ideas of what they would like to do with free time, when they would like input and discussion times, what kind of worship they'd like, etc. Many classes have been able to completely plan and carry through morning and evening devotions, Sunday worship services, music and gab fests, and other sessions. Skits and games are usually fun for teenagers to plan, and the more students who become involved in planning and executing these activities, the better "into it" they will be as a group. Give them guidance and helpful suggestions but also allow them the freedom and creativity to "do their own thing."

Bring along what you will need

Although this is not the structured setting you have normally used, you will need to check out what equipment and supplies will be available and what you will need to supply in order to carry out the plans you've made. Film projectors, screens, record players, recreational equipment, paper, pencils, marking pens, poster board, newspapers and/or magazines, pizza cutters, popcorn popper, chalk, tape recorder—whatever is needed for your time to be used as you want it, should be brought with you if they are not part of the retreat equipment.

Encourage fellowship, family, and fun

One of the things the course stresses as a regular classroom priority is caring and concern for one another. A number of activities and projects are planned specifically to allow students to experiment in becoming friends, sharing with each other and learning to relate as Christians in a caring way. You can do this at a retreat by encouraging students to include others in their walks, eat with someone they've not sat by before pick a partner they don't know well, etc. Small chores could be assigned by pairs to help build relationships, such as setting the table, filling milk pitchers, or cleaning floors. If opportunities are built in for exposing young people to one another, many will come to know someone they had not "discovered" before. They will have fun together and learn about each other at the same time.

Relax and enjoy it

Some of our greatest experiences can be the unplanned, unrehearsed, and unexpected. Being together for a longer period of time with your class can put pressure on you to perform if you let it. But you can carry out your plans and still relax and enjoy it if you allow yourself enough time. Try to be free enough about what happens so you can go through the retreat relaxed and ready for what comes. You must be yourself if the students are going to be themselves. You are there to retreat too—let yourself have fun, unwind, get time alone—whatever you need to enjoy it.

Model retreat

In order to show how the material in this course can be used in a retreat setting, a model retreat will be described, based on Chapters 17-19 of the course. A schedule is provided for the model retreat; then various elements of the retreat schedule are described in detail.

Model retreat schedule

Friday

5:00 P.M.	Leave church, possible dinner stop
8:00 P.M.	Arrive at retreat center, unpack, make beds, put equipment where it is accessible, free time to explore the grounds or facilities
9:00 P.M.	Discovery session 1: "The Story of God's Love, Part 2"
10:00 P.M.	Lounge time, pizza party, music, and relaxation
10:45 P.M.	Clean-up
11:00 P.M.	Evening devotions
11:15 P.M.	Lights out

Saturday

8:00 A.M.	Rise and shine
8:45 A.M.	Morning devotions
9:00 A.M.	Breakfast
9:45 A.M.	Discovery session 2: "Death to King Jesus"
11:30 A.M.	Free time
Noon	Lunch
1:00 P.M.	Recreation, skit planning
4:00 P.M.	Creative project time
5:00 P.M.	Discovery session 3: "Long Live King Jesus"
6:00 P.M.	Dinner
6:30 P.M.	Free time, games, music, chat groups
8:00 P.M.	Celebration and happening hour
9:30 P.M.	Break, popcorn and soda, music
10:00 P.M.	Movies
11:45 P.M.	Evening devotions
Midnight	Lights out

Sunday

8:00 A.M.	Rise and shine
8:45 A.M.	Morning devotions
9:00 A.M.	Breakfast
10:00 A.M.	Worship service
11:00 A.M.	Free time, sharing groups, games, music
Noon	Lunch
1:00 P.M.	Evaluation, sharing
2:00 P.M.	Leave retreat center
5:00 P.M.	Arrive back at church

Planning suggestions for using model retreat

Now let's get down some specifics about what to do in the scheduled study sessions at a retreat. It is understood that this section is only a guide to help you establish your own pattern for a retreat. The number of chapters in the course which you wish to cover would depend on the duration of your retreat, the number of hours of study you want to schedule, and how you want to approach the material. Scheduling will also be affected by the nature of your group. Stay flexible and open to suggestions.

It is important that you *assign the reading* of the chapters to be covered *before* going on the retreat. When information goes home about cost, what to bring, etc., make a note for families that students need to bring their books, Bibles, and should have read *all* the chapters indicated. Remind them again shortly before the retreat that this assignment needs to be done.

Model session plan

The main opportunities for learning the material you want to cover can be called discovery sessions. In the model one is scheduled for Friday evening, one for Saturday morning, and one for Saturday afternoon. During these times you will have a chance to study Chapters 17-19 and add any discussion or activities which will help in teaching these three lessons. Basic input of information and content should come during these times.

In addition, there are other activities during the retreat which you can use to emphasize a certain idea or event in other ways. For instance, devotions and Sunday worship can use the same basic content; skit planning and creative project time can also pick up on ideas connected with these lessons.

Read back through the chapters in the front part of this guide. On pages 65-73 you will find background information and ideas for getting into the content material. Adapt what is feasible and interesting to you and innovate your own ideas for activities you would not be able to use in the classroom setting at home.

Discovery session 1

Material to be covered: Chapter 17—"The Story of God's Love, Part 2."

Session overview and suggestions. Because this is the first discovery session, take a few minutes to introduce what it is we are planing to cover in the material during this retreat.

Turn to the reading books and allow the students to refresh their memories about the lessons they have had during the first half of the year. Move into an open discussion about the three chapters they have read for this retreat by asking some questions about where this story is now leading us. Give the students a few minutes to review Chapter 17 before getting into the specific lesson we are talking about.

While the students review the chapter, put up a time line of the Bible (similar to the one in the book) on a large piece of poster board. If you can collect a number of pictures about continuing stories such as comic book characters (Superman, Little Orphan Annie, Dick Tracy, cowboy heroes), post these around the room. Spread among them any pictures you can find of characters in our story such as Moses, David, Joseph, or Noah.

Discussion of the chapter could include talking about any stories the students recall which have a *continued* kind of emphasis. The point is for them to get the idea that the Old and New Testaments are telling *one continuous story* of God and his people. The individual characters and events in the story may come and go, but the story is still going on.

If you brought some comic books or pictures of such stories, students can no doubt identify them and the stories about them. Ask them to identify things that are constant or recurring themes in these stories. They might say things like, "Superman always wins." Can they identify some things that are constant or recurring about the story of the Bible?

We can see that there are really many chapters (or books) in this story (the Bible). Can they remember how many books are found within the Bible? Looking at your Bibles, list on the board how many books are in the Old and New Testament. What different kinds of books can they recall we found in the Old Testament? Write their answers on the board (*poetry, history, prophecy*).

Can they list some of the main characters or events of the first part of our story? Do they see some of them pictured around the room? Can they add any from the chapter that will begin the part of the story that we find in the New Testament? They may name Matthew, Mark, Luke, John, or Paul. Write on slips of paper the people or events they are naming. Give each student one slip of paper. Ask them to arrange themselves around the room in order as they come in history. This will work all right for most Old Testament characters, but not necessarily for those who come from the New Testament. If they don't recognize this difficulty, point out that the books of the New Testament are not printed in the order in which they were written.

This should open the idea that the New Testament is not as easy to place in historical sequence. It deals more with subjects than time—and with a *central event* in the life of the main character (the cross and the resurrection).

Indicate that this primary concern is why the gospels are placed where they are in the New Testament —although they may not have been written first. The main message of the story is in them. Jesus, his life, death, and resurrection are what the whole story depends on!

Describe a savior. An activity would be good which gives students a chance to review the types of Messiah the people of Jesus' day were looking for and the kind we sometimes expect now.

Ask each student to write down one type of Messiah or deliverer expected at the time Jesus came. Then suggest they write a paragraph about what type of savior they feel we need today, trying to zero in on one quality or characteristic most needed. They might think of a peacemaker, lawmaker, preacher, reformer, etc.

Share ideas about what a savior should be—and what people expected of God's Messiah. Discuss what our chapter says about this.

Optional activities

1. You could have the class work on a mural depicting the theme of the one continuous story that is told in the Bible, showing characters and events we've covered and emphasizing what is central in the story. Provide a large roll of shelf or butcher paper and felt-tip markers and ask every class member to help.

2. Dramatize the story or parts of it, asking students to choose characters that played a part in the story. Try to tell in a short role play the main theme of the Bible through these roles, and especially how they are tied together.

3. "Popcorn" prayer (see page 49) would be a good ending for this session. Suggest they think about specific people or events that played a part in this one continuous story we've talked about. Begin by naming one or two and thanking God for using them as part of his story.

4. Symbols for key people and events could be drawn and colored and hung around the retreat center as reminders that we are part of the story—we are "surrounded by a cloud of witnesses" (Heb. 12:1).

Discovery session 2

Material to be covered: Chapter 18—"Death to King Jesus."

Session overview and suggestions. You are dealing here with the subject of death, with the cross and Jesus' death being the central event of our story. It is important also to deal with the subject in terms of each of us, as the fundamental experience of brokenness. Reread all the material in Chapter 18 and in the teacher's guide on pages 68 through 70, particularly the background information. Give some minutes for reviewing the chapter and biblical material contained within it.

Write on the board: *Why is there death? Where is God in all this?* Discuss the chapter and what they feel it says about death, beginning with the idea of Jesus' death, or with the idea of everybody dying, whichever comes up first.

Ask why people die. Help the students discuss the idea that no matter what the various causes are, everybody dies. The real tragedy is not cancer, car accidents, or old age, bad as they are. A broken relationship with God is much more tragic because of its destructive effects during life and after—and because Jesus had to die to restore this broken relationship.

Optional activities

1. Ask the students to write their own wills. Young people do not often think seriously about their own death, or prepare for it. What would they want done, what last things would they say to loved ones, what would they leave to certain people, etc. Share feelings about doing this writing, if not specifics of what is written.

2. Look at Jesus' death. Use the chapter and the biblical material describing both the Old Testament prophecy and New Testament fulfillment, found on pages 112-116 in the student book. Review the fact that this death was the final proof that God is in charge: even in death God enters and does something about it himself.

3. Write questions about death. Give students a chance to ask specific questions they've had, sharing personal fears or experiences, and talk together about common worries and fears regarding death. If your pastor is along, let him collect these questions, read, and lead a discussion on these questions, sharing information he has about the church's position and the Bible's words to us. If he is not present you may want to talk with him about this matter so you will be prepared to lead the discussion.

4. Write poetry. Students can share their feelings and beliefs through poems about Jesus' death and our own experience with it. Suggest they concentrate on their own feelings and what God has done in Jesus about death. Let any who wish share what they have written or talk about it.

5. Plan a funeral service. Young people often have good ideas for what should be said and done at a funeral. Ask them to share music and sermon suggestions, choose hymns and other songs appropriate to our beliefs, and prescribe other things such as where, when, and how it should be conducted.

In all of these activities, keep in mind that the happy ending to the death story is our lesson for later today—the resurrection! Don't let depression slip over the group—keep foremost God's personal involvement in death and his victory in Jesus.

Be sure to choose activities on the basis of what might interest your group and work well with them—and limit the activities so that they can be done well rather than having too many unfinished projects.

Discovery session 3

Material to be covered: Chapter 19—"Long Live King Jesus!"

Session overview and suggestions. Here's the happy ending to the lesson we had earlier about death and God's victory through Jesus. The resurrection is the proof and celebration that God has overcome evil. We are all included in this victory over death—God has kept his promise to send a Savior.

Don't worry if you can't answer every question about death and resurrection—no one else has done it either! Keep in mind this is an important and fundamental event of our faith, so we shouldn't be surprised that there are deep concepts and unanswered questions coming up.

Read again the material in this guide covering Chapter 19, on pages 71-73. Give the students a few minutes again for reviewing the chapter and biblical material. Discuss the chapter with plenty of time for their own impressions and comments about Jesus' resurrection—do they think it really happened? What does it mean for each of us? Can we believe in a resurrection? What questions do they have about it?

Optional activities

1. Easter art. Using poster board, egg cartons or egg-shaped containers, tissue paper, yarn, cloth scraps, pipe cleaners, tempera or water-color paints, what can the students make to depict the idea of resurrection? Consider doing clay sculpture if you have the materials and time.

2. Taped narrative. Assign roles in the Easter story and ask the students to retell it as though it were happening now and we were taping it live for a news show on a local TV station. Write the dialog only if you feel it is necessary; otherwise, let them improvise.

Actually tape what is said in interviewing the eye witnesses at Easter and play it back. See the lesson helps on pages 71 and 72 in this guide.

3. The resurrected body—Bible study. Go back into the chapter and your Bibles searching for clues to what Jesus looked like. How did people recognize him? How can we describe Jesus after the resurrection? What things do we notice are the same or different? What do we mean when we say Jesus becomes known to us in word and in sacrament? Is there evidence of this? Look at the last chapter of the gospels especially.

4. Plan an Easter service. If you have not already used the idea of the funeral service it might be exciting to let the group plan a service for your congregation as though it were Easter. How about using it as your Sunday worship service? Assign one or more to give the sermon, with help from the group; pick the hymns, other music, lessons, any special drama or storytelling, etc.

5. Make triptychs. This is a three-sided art piece which can be made by cutting poster board in folding parts. The center picture carries the main idea or theme, the two side panels use ideas or symbols that point to the center or are offshoots of it. This could be done during creativity time instead. (See Chapter 6 for a drawing of a triptych.)

Other retreat activity times can be used for emphasizing the material in these study sessions. Try to lead the group with suggestions and ideas that can help them reinforce the topics and learning of these chapters. They may also be willing to offer suggestions, perhaps recalling activities from other retreats.

Applying this material
Devotions

Our proposed schedule calls for four occasions when the group has a 15-minute period of devotions. This can be done in an informal and easy manner and need not be greatly structured or polished in form. Young people themselves can be in charge—it might be a good idea to divide the entire group into four small groups, suggesting that they each plan one devotional time for the whole class. One leader could work with them as a resource person, staying in the background but assisting when necessary.

Students should be encouraged to use Scripture, prayer, music, and witness in any way they feel appropriate. The topic or theme they use could relate to the material we are studying in the three discovery sessions, picking up one specific point of a lesson, or combining several. They should keep it simple and include as many of the total group in participation as possible.

Skit planning

The idea of small groups would again be helpful—it might be good to have different small groups for this activity. Suggest they each plan one skit that is humorous, just for laughs, and one skit that is biblical. This could be a story we have studied, one that is coming up, a parable, or a miracle, but they are to read it from the Bible, redo it any way they like, and present it to the group at the "Celebration and Happening Hour" on Saturday night.

Creative project time

You can use activities suggested under the discovery session plans that you did not have time for to fill this hour. Or think up some other kinds of projects that give the young people a chance to be creative and imaginative. Here are some suggestions:

1. Write a letter to one of the Bible characters, telling what you learned about this person from the biblical account, giving advice or comment on it.

2. Make a gift of some sort to present to the group during evaluation and sharing time, which tells something about what you have been given by the group.

3. Draw a symbol of yourself and share it with the group at evaluation and sharing time. It should be positive in nature and true.

Celebration and happening hour

This is a chance for the kids to goof off for one another—to use their talents, laugh together, and in general enjoy life. Skits, songs, general hilarity is the idea.

Sunday worship service

This can be worked on before you leave for the retreat, or it can be assigned to a small group as their project while they are there. It has already been suggested that it could be an outgrowth of one of the discovery sessions. Try to involve the young people themselves in leadership roles in the service, with teachers as resource people during planning.

Evaluation and sharing

Consider giving the group paper and pencils and five minutes to write "What I liked best about this retreat." Then share the results. You could also use this time for projects that haven't been used, creative efforts some might have missed, etc. Listen to the students evaluate what happened not only in the discovery sessions, but all the time the retreat was in progress. Telling what has happened in their relationships with one another can be valuable. Summarizing all that has happened and all we've meant to each other is an excellent preparation for going home.

Other retreats

The retreat model given above for Chapters 17-19 shows how a retreat can be organized around the materials in this course. Following are suggested unit divisions for the rest of the course, with a few ideas for activities. These could be used as suggested in the model or modified as you wish.

Suggested unit divisions for retreats

Old Testament		New Testament	
Unit 1	Chapters 1-5	Unit 5	Chapters 17-19
Unit 2	Chapters 6-9	Unit 6	Chapters 20-24
	(or Chapter 9 could go into Unit 3)	Unit 7	Chapters 25-28 (or Chapter 28 could go into Unit 8)
Unit 3	Chapters 10-13		
Unit 4	Chapters 14-16		
		Unit 8	Chapters 29-32

Suggested retreat activities for each unit

Important! Always reread the material in the lesson section of this guide for each chapter included in the unit you're covering.

Unit 1   Chapters 1-5

1. Draw a picture of the Bible's theme. Decide what you think is the main point of the story in the Bible and try to depict it in symbol or characters. Then write in one phrase the theme you picked for the Bible.

2. Make a map tracing the journey Abraham took when God called him to a new land. Color and mark all important countries, cities, rivers, etc.

3. Make a patriarch tree. Make a family tree of the characters we've studied in these chapters. Begin with Abraham and mark in red his descendants who carried on God's promise.

4. Creation pieces. Make a banner or collage about the kind of world God created. Gather materials from the retreat area and include them in a nature nest or collection.

5. Write a diary page or letter as though you were Abraham writing to friends left behind at his old home before God called him to the land of promise. Describe what has happened to God's promise and any feelings Abraham might have had along the way.

6. Make a list of key words from this unit and what they mean. Share them with the group. Include words like *covenant* and *chosen*.

7. Play the Game of Life described in Chapter 4, setting up teams and prizes for the winners.

Unit 2   Chapters 6-9

1. Use the movie *Exodus* and discuss this latter-day exodus along with the biblical story of God's people and the land he gives them.

2. Role play the life of Moses in three main parts: (1) his birth and recovery as a baby from the Nile; (2) his work as a shepherd and the call from God; and (3) his leading the people out of Egypt and the giving of the law.

3. Discuss the kinds of laws talked about in Chapter 7 and the kinds of laws we live under today—the groups, clubs, people, we belong to that have rules.

4. Using the chart in Chapter 9, draw up a list of qualifications for being king in biblical times. Then draw up your own list of qualifications for a king or president now.

5. Draw symbols for each of the kings we read about in Chapter 9 and explain why you used that particular symbol.

Unit 3   Chapters 10-13

1. Write poetry about things that happened during the time discussed in these chapters, especially about the feelings of the people at this time.

2. Describe the prophets of repentance and the prophets of promise and hope. Compare what they had to say to the people, and when and why they came when they did.

3. Make repentance cycles as described in Chapter 11 and talk about the need to repent and how God is able to change us when we are willing to change.

4. Plan an exile experience like the one in Chapter 12, using the retreat facilities to heighten the feeling of disorientation and not belonging. Discuss the problems of being away from home and any experiences students have had with this.

5. Discuss nations that have grown to power, divided, and fallen. Talk about the problems of divisions within a country, the need for leadership, and the difficulties God's people had at this time.

Unit 4   Chapters 14-16

1. Research and rebuild a replica of the temple—similar to the project facing the people on their return from exile. Study what it was like; make a scale model.

2. Write songs and poetry similar to that studied in Chapter 15. Use music and whatever resource materials you have, trying to get the idea of human response to our experience with God.

3. Plan a worship service of the original music, poetry, songs, etc., that you come up with during this study. Or use psalms, songs, and poems found in the Bible as the basis for devotions and tell how they come to be in the Bible and what we learned about these human responses.

4. Present a news show about the return from the exile. Interview people who left and are coming home, some who were born away, etc. Tell their feelings of not belonging, and of coming back. Describe the job

of rebuilding, and report their explanation for the problems the people were having.

5. Run a "show of shows," highlighting heroes of the Old Testament. Select an emcee and ask students to play the hero they most admire, allowing each a two-minute speech about his or her life. Have each tell who motivated the actions and events that are reported in the Bible. For a twist, give the audience score cards that are numbered, then have the heroes tell their stories without giving a name and award a prize to the participant guessing the most heroes.

Unit 5   Chapters 17-19

This unit was used as the retreat model at the beginning of this section—see pages 124-126 for details.

Unit 6   Chapters 20-24

1. Do a "This Is Your Life" on John the Baptist. Bring into his scrapbook the biblical characters surrounding his birth, his parents, his growing up (what was he like as a teenager?), and his ministry calling people to repentance. People who take part would talk about him from their character's viewpoint. Research what you can from the Bible and imagine his personality and environment from what we read there.

2. Hold a forum about the four gospels, described in Chapter 20. Discuss why we benefit from having four different gospel accounts.

3. Prepare skits on the four miracles presented in Chapter 21, page 78. Ask the students to retell these stories and portray the characters in them as though it were happening now. Show how they would react and feel, and what it means to follow Jesus today.

4. After discussing Chapter 22 and the biblical parables, have the students try to write modern-day parables. They should choose their own ideas, issues, and characters which would fit into modern life and values. Have them select their own important points for each story, write them in, and share them aloud.

5. Do an art project about the miracles or the parables. Suggest they try to depict one main idea from these chapters in a collage, sculpture, painting or drawing. Hold an art fair if you like, displaying pieces that deal with Jesus' teaching and miracles. Have each artist talk about his or her piece.

6. Write poetry about Jesus under the heading, "Who do you say that I am?" These should be personal feelings and experiences. What do the students think about him?

Unit 7   Chapters 25-28

1. Run a campaign for "Jesus Christ for President." Let the students pick themes, songs, prepare banners, posters, write speeches, listen to music about him, trying to convince people why he should be our leader.

2. Plan a celebration, a birthday party for the church. Study again the Pentecost story in Chapter 26 and arrange to retell the story of the great day when the church was "born." Invite people who were there to retell what happened and what it means to us.

3. Make banners about witnessing for Jesus, the church, and the work of the Holy Spirit.

4. Plan witness projects your class can carry out during the year. Discuss ways you can be witnesses. Check the field trip suggestions in Chapter 27 of this guide, page 98. Get students to think of ideas and write them on the board, then select which ones would be best for your group and lay out details about what you will do, when, how.

5. Hold a contest on the chapters covered during the retreat, asking students to draw up questions and answers, dividing the group into two teams and awarding prizes (first in line for dinner?) to the winning team.

Unit 8   Chapters 29-32

1. Do a "This Is Your Life" for Paul, similar to the one suggested for John the Baptist under Unit 6. (Be sure to backtrack into Chapter 28.)

2. Plan a missionary journey as though you were going today. Where would the followers of Paul and Jesus go to spread the gospel now? What would you take along, what would you say, what problems would you expect, and how would you overcome them?

3. Make mobiles on the theme of grace as described in Chapter 30, page 107. If you want to enlarge the theme, include Paul's life and travels, the idea of grace in our life today, and whatever other ideas your students pick up from these chapters studied.

4. Use a film about Christian freedom and responsibility to emphasize ideas in Chapter 31. After the showing discuss how we feel about and relate to the picture. Talk about our own experiences with both freedom and responsibility.

5. Do creative writing about the end of the world and the return of Jesus. Think about how you will feel, what it will be like, things we know and don't know, etc. Write your feelings about it and share the writing as a group after studying Chapter 32.

6. The gift-giving activity described in Chapter 32 is an excellent retreat activity. It gives opportunity for positive and personal exchanges between students.

7. Hold an evaluation seminar discussing the year's materials and the class's experience with them. Write and talk about what was studied, what we learned, and how we worked together as a group. Did the students have objectives in mind as they began? Did they reach any of these? What benefits did the class bring to individuals? What suggestions for improvement for next year can be made?

www.ingramcontent.com/pod-product-compliance
Lightning Source LLC
Chambersburg PA
CBHW082249300426
44110CB00039B/2493